SHOW UP AND LEAD

Unlock the Power of Self-Awareness and Be Your Best Self at Work

TurtlePublishing

Copyright © 2025 Dr Nancy Bonfiglio-Pavisich

The information in these modules is based on the author's experiences, opinions and research. While every effort has been made to ensure its accuracy at the date of publication/circulation, this material is of a general, educational nature and is guidance only. It should not be interpreted as legal or other specific advice, nor should it be taken as being completely free of error or omission. As this material may not necessarily be a fully comprehensive coverage of any topic nor cover all specific situations. Before acting or relying upon any of the information in this material, you should seek appropriate professional and or legal advice in regards to your specific circumstances.

The author and publisher disclaims responsibility for any adverse consequences, which may result from the use of the information therein.

All rights reserved. No part of this publication may be reproduced, stored in or introduced into a retrieval system, or transmitted in any form, or by any means (electronic, mechanical, photocopying, recording or otherwise) without the prior written permission of the author. Any person who does any unauthorised acts in relation to this publication will be liable to criminal prosecution and civil claims for damages.

First published by Turtle Publishing 2025

Cover & Illustrations by Turtle Publishing

turtlepublishing.com.au

Personal Note

I dedicate this book to all the incredible clients I have had the privilege of working with. You're all true leaders. Leadership isn't defined by a title but by the actions you take to improve yourself, grow and support others, and make the world a better place. Your achievements are a testament to your commitment to these values. I'm in awe of your determination and dedication. Your integrity, skill, and courage have been a great source of inspiration. Thank you.

This book highlights these qualities and serves as a reminder of your greatness. Thank you for being a part of this journey.

I also want to acknowledge Dr Ross James, an incredible human being with the patience of a saint. Last, but not least, I deeply thank my husband Mark and daughters Jacinta and Kascia. Thank you for all that you have done to enable me to fulfil another dream. I love you all.

About the Author

Dr Nancy Bonfiglio-Pavisich is a consultant specialising in leadership, management, and communication. She is the Director of Reframe WA Consulting and lives by the motto *review, renew, and regenerate*. Nancy is a passionate educator and facilitator who works with individuals, teams, and organisations to develop their respective leadership, management, and communication capacities.

Using evidence-based research, including neuroscience, coupled with mentoring and coaching, Nancy provides individual consultations, creates bespoke programs, facilitates workshops, and speaks publicly to support all stakeholders' personal and professional growth.

As a multi-award winner, Nancy has received an ACEL New Voice Scholarship Award (2020) and has been recognised with a Certificate of Excellence in Educational Leadership (2021) in Western Australia (ACELWA). Nancy's research has also seen her awarded A Western Australian Institute for Educational Research Award for Mentoring (2022) and an ACEL Fellowship Award in 2022.

Contents

Introduction   xi

How do I Turn Up?

Self-Awareness   3
What is the self?   4
What is self-awareness?   5
Why am I sharing this research with you?   8
What does it mean to be self-aware?   9
What are the effects of self-awareness?   12
What do leaders and managers say
about self-awareness?   12
What can you do to build your self-awareness?   14

Values   21
What are values?   22
Workplace values   26
Core values in the workplace   27

Emotional Intelligence   33
What are emotions?   36
What is emotional intelligence?   37
How to review, renew and regenerate
emotional intelligence in the workplace   39
Why is emotional intelligence so
important for leaders in workplaces?   41

Resilience   47
What is resilience?   49
What is resilience in the workplace
from an individual perspective?   50
What is resilience in the workplace
from a team perspective?   54

How Do Others See You Turn Up?

Engagement at Work   65
What is engagement?   67
What is employee/colleague engagement?   67
Employee/colleague engagement   70
Rewards and recognition   72
Empowering employees   73
Building a bond between employees and leaders   74

Accountability at Work   77
What is accountability?   78
Trust   81
Quality feedback   82
Solution-focused   82
What is the difference between
accountability and responsibility?   84
What happens when there's a lack of
accountability?   85
Workplace accountability tools   85

Quality Decision-Making   91
Decision-making tools   93
How do you prevent bias in decision-making?   98

Leadership with Integrity, Skill and Courage   105
Leadership as behaviour   106
Leadership as a way of being   113

Call to Action

Tools and Techniques   121
Self-awareness   121
Values   124
Emotional intelligence   126
Resilience   128
Engagement and motivation   130
Accountability   131
Decision-making   132
Bringing it all together   133

Endnotes   *137*
Bibliography   *143*
For Further Reading   *155*

Introduction

Welcome to *Show Up and Lead*. I'm here to guide you on a journey of self-discovery, to assist you in understanding how you can best 'show up' at work. You see, the way we perceive ourselves and how we appear can sometimes be quite different. We all like to think of ourselves as kind individuals who support those around us, but the reality might not always align with our self-perception.

In my workshops, I begin with two questions: *How do you show up?* and *How do others see you show up?* Initially, participants often focus on the physical aspects of their presence, such as being well-dressed, clean and prepared for the day. But when I invite them to delve deeper, they start to reveal more about their emotional state – whether they're feeling distracted, rushed, stressed, or positive and energetic. Recognising these aspects is crucial to understanding how we show up, not just for ourselves but for others as well.

Let me share a story from a recent workshop. I met Janice, a career-focused accountant with three school-aged children and a partner who regularly travels for work. When asked *How do you show up?* Janice initially focused on her appearance – her makeup, hair, attire. But when prodded, she shared a detailed account of her morning routine. She starts her day super-early, gets herself ready, packs her bag, then embarks on the journey of getting her children out of bed, feeding them breakfast, making lunches, and getting them to two different schools by half-past eight. This is on a good day when all the children are healthy and there are no major challenges. When things go wrong, they really go wrong.

Janice realised that she shows up at work as two different people depending on how her morning goes. On good days, she's able to handle challenges that come her way. However, on stressful days, her lack of clarity and frustration not only affect her work but also how she connects with people.

This situation isn't unusual. We all face challenges getting to work in the morning – whether it's taking care of our beloved pets, ensuring our loved ones are okay or navigating traffic.

What matters here is our awareness of self. What do we need to do more of, or less of, to be the best version of ourselves with integrity, skill[1] and with courage?

This book is divided into three parts. The first explores how we show up for work. The second examines how others see us show up for work. The third part invites a call to action.

How do we show up for work? invites us to explore self-awareness. We often talk about being self-aware, but are we really? We'll look at relevant research and examine how we can apply this learning to our situations. And we also explore the power of our unconscious biases, our growth mindsets and our resilience capacity

How others see us show up for work challenges us to consider the provocations that impact how we show up for others. We'll explore concepts such as empathy, engagement verses motivation, accountability, decision-making and being of service to others.

Part three, the call to action, invites us to consider several strategies that help us to show up more effectively for ourselves and others. This is the practical element of the book so take the time to examine specific strategies that will assist you to show up at work in a way that aligns with your ideal self-perception and that enables you to be your best self.

So let's embark on this journey of self-discovery together.

I have written this book as a follow-up to the feedback received from my first book, *It's All About IT! Evidence-based, practical guide to workplace communications*. In that book, I encouraged readers to focus on the behaviour of a person and not them personally. In this book, I challenge you to think about what you can do to show up for yourself and others in a way that honours dignity at home and at work.

In a constantly evolving world, we must show up as our best selves, even on challenging days. I invite you to consider the mantra of being ourselves with integrity, skill and courage. We become better versions of ourselves professionally and personally when we act with integrity, use our skills to the best of our ability, and have the courage to face challenges.

Integrity unlocks the benefits of self-awareness and transparency. It's the foundation of emotional intelligence and resilience, empowering us to form deep connections with others. We can build stronger relationships and cultivate a supportive work environment when we truly understand ourselves.

Skill is the engine that drives team success. It empowers us to engage and motivate our colleagues, make informed decisions, and communicate effectively. By honing our skills, we ensure our contributions are valuable and impactful, propelling the team towards success.

Courage is the catalyst for fostering a safe and open work environment. It allows us to be vulnerable, empathetic, and authentic. It means embracing our true selves and encouraging others to do the same. Courage in the workplace is the cornerstone of an environment where everyone feels safe to express their ideas and take risks.

By integrating these three principles, we practice leadership in its truest form. Leadership is not about holding a title but about guiding and inspiring others. We engage in leadership when we show up with integrity, skill and courage. And that is why I encourage you to consider the concept of *Show Up and Lead* like this:

- Be you with *integrity*
- Be you with *skill*
- Be you with *courage*

PART 1

How do I Turn Up?

Chapter One

Self-Awareness

• • •

The Journey of the Horse and the Rider

The story of the Horse and the Rider illustrates the human experience through the metaphor of two companions: the Horse, representing our emotional, instinctive brain, and the Rider, symbolising our logical, cognitive perspective. The Horse, driven by deep feelings and ancient instincts, often veers onto its own path, while the Rider, despite holding the reins and planning the course, struggles

to steer when emotions surge. This dynamic creates a constant tug-of-war between reason and raw emotion, highlighting the challenges of balancing our emotional impulses with rational thought.

The message of the story emphasises the importance of harmony between our emotional and rational selves. The Horse's passionate nature reminds us of the beauty of feeling deeply, while the Rider's intellect keeps us on track. To navigate life's complexities, we must be aware of how we balance these forces, honouring both the wild, emotional Horse and the strategic, thoughtful Rider. This balance fosters self-awareness and helps us understand others, as we all seek equilibrium on our unique journeys.

• • •

What is the self?

We often discuss self-awareness, but what does it mean to be self-aware? There are numerous theories that define self. Social researchers and anthropologists argue that the self is a product of our social experiences and relationships.

Research suggests that there are many diverse perspectives on what constitutes self-awareness. One perspective divides the research on the self into two parts. The first part focuses on self-linked social processes and communication that draw inspiration from observing others. The second part explores the self as a complex entity that consists of conscious and subconscious layers. Julia Carden and colleagues (who are experts in management and organisational behaviour) reviewed published studies and articles about self-awareness and concluded that self is defined as 'multidimensional, made up of both conscious and unconscious layers, and heavily influenced by observations of others'.[2]

What is self-awareness?

Self awareness is the ability to recognise who you are; your values; beliefs and the boundaries that define you as a person. Being clear about these factors means that you are aware of how independent you are from others.[3]

Our own sense of self-awareness is influenced by context and developed over time by the experiences we have as well as any motivation we have to want to do and be better. In the review I mentioned earlier, Carden and her colleagues confirmed that understanding self is a process of first, self-awareness, then self-consciousness, and the final aspect of understanding self is self-knowledge. They identified three meta-themes of self-awareness in management and education that are summarised in the following three figures that I have modified a little. The three themes identified in the figures below are: how self-awareness is classified, how to be self-aware, and the purpose of self-awareness.

The classification of self-awareness as intrapersonal refers to an internal mindset. Interpersonal self-awareness involves understanding our influence on others. Obviously, a person can have a combination of both.

Classifications of Self-Awareness

Intrapersonal   Interpersonal   Both

How can a person be self-aware? The first aspect, which is self-evaluation and self-reflection, involves being mindful of how others perceive you. The second aspect is called process because the discovery of self is a dynamic and ongoing experience. Attention, the final aspect of being self-aware, emphasises the importance of the focus and effort that are needed to create self-awareness.

How to be Self-Aware

Self-Evaluation   Process   Attention

By blending our understanding of self and awareness as separate concepts, we learn about self. One purpose of self-awareness is to develop the way we perceive ourselves. Another purpose of self-awareness is to understand our behaviour and how we interact with others. Paying attention to how we turn up and treat others helps us improve our thoughts and actions.

Purpose of Self-Awareness

Learn about self   Learn about impact on others

When we see ourselves clearly, we become more aware of who we are and how we interact with our surroundings. Such clarity generates increased confidence and creativity, which allows us to connect better with others, to make well-informed decisions, and to foster better relationships.

The developmental psychologist, Philippe Rochat, identified five levels of self-awareness between birth and five years of age.[4] The first, differentiation, is the phase when an infant can recognise their reflection. It's a crucial milestone for further development. The second level is referred to as the situation, which refers to a child's awareness about their action in a particular situation when the child can connect their actions to their environment. Often, this is referred to as foundational to their capacity to engage with the world. In the third stage, identification, children can identify self, or *me*. It forms the platform for the formation of the concept of self. The fourth level occurs when children can recognise themselves in images despite changes in growth. The final stage is self-consciousness. In this stage, children are cognisant of how they are perceived by others, which is why they focus on being accepted by others. This is crucial because it forms the foundation of social development and our life journey.

Why am I sharing this research with you?

Although we understand that self-awareness is constantly changing, we may not always recognise how it affects our personal growth and relationships with others. As Charles Taylor notes in his book, *Sources of the Self*: 'What we are constantly losing from sight is that being a self is inseparable from existing in a space of moral issues, to do with identity and how one ought to be. It is finding one's standpoint in this space and occupying a perspective in it.'[5]

What does it mean to be self-aware?

The review of self-awareness studies by Carden et al. identified the process of understanding self (self-awareness, self-consciousness and self-knowledge) and they described three meta-themes of self-awareness (classifications of self-awareness, how to be self-aware and the purpose of self-awareness).

However, Dr Tasha Eurich, an organisational psychologist, conducted a large-scale scientific study of self-awareness. She undertook 10 separate investigations with nearly 5000 participants to investigate what self-awareness really is, why it is needed, and how it can be increased in the workplace.[6]

Surprisingly, Eurich found that only 10 to 15 percent of the participants were self-aware and were able to maintain quality relationships because of their self-awareness. Two broad categories of self-awareness emerged.

- **Internal self-awareness** is all about understanding our values, actions, strengths and weaknesses, and how they affect those around us. These people tend to experience greater satisfaction in the workplace and relationships; they tend to be happier because they feel more in control of their lives.

- **External self-awareness** is about understanding how others view or perceive us. People with this knowledge tend to be better at showing empathy and comprehending others' perspectives.

Eurich mapped four self-awareness archetypes against internal and external self-awareness: introspectors, aware, seekers and pleasers.

- **Introspectors** had high internal self-awareness because they knew who they were, and low external self-awareness because they didn't seek feedback about their impact on others.

- **Aware** individuals were strong in both internal and external self-awareness because they were self-confident and open to learning more about themselves from others.

- **Seekers** were unclear about who they were (low internal self-awareness) and because of this, were challenged by their relationship with others (low external awareness).

- **Pleasers** were eager to support others (high external self-awareness) at the cost of self (low self-awareness).

Self-Awareness Archetypes

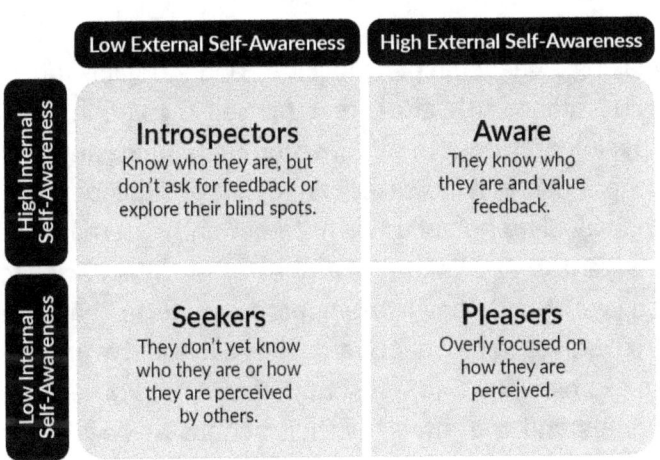

Sometimes introspection doesn't lead to improved self-awareness. According to Eurich's research, some people who engage in introspection are less self-aware and tend to report lower job satisfaction and wellbeing. The problem arises when people engage in the process incorrectly. As human beings, we may believe that we have a complete understanding of the reasons behind our actions, but in reality, we don't have access to our subconscious thoughts, feelings and emotions. That is why it's better to ask *What?* instead of *Why?* For instance, rather than ask *Why isn't this working for me?* we should ask *What situation isn't working for me?*

What are the effects of self-awareness?

Self-awareness contributes to more effective decision-making, leadership capacity and organisational performance. It's also great for self-regulation (we'll speak more about this in Chapter 2) and being aware of others' needs. It increases confidence and competence. Individuals who focus on internal and external self-awareness are more likely to seek feedback, to engage in a lifelong learning process, and to challenge themselves to move forward. They can use this process to examine how they present themselves to others and understand the effect of their actions at each point along the way.

What do leaders and managers say about self-awareness?

Satya Nadella – CEO of Microsoft
Satya Nadella, who became CEO of Microsoft in 2014, believes self-awareness is critical for individuals and their organisations. Nadella changed the way

Microsoft's culture worked by emphasising teamwork, open-mindedness and quality discussions. In order to create a good workplace culture, it's important to know your purpose and make sure it lines up with what you value and enjoy.[7]

Arianna Huffington – Huff Post
Arianna Huffington is well known for establishing the *Huffington Post* as a global newspaper. After a personal crisis, she became very aware of wellbeing with a strong lens on self-awareness. A personal and professional reassessment of her life, daily introspection and the way in which she subsequently reframed how she lived her life became essential to being more self-aware.

Brené Brown – Research Professor
In a fascinating interview, Brené Brown, a research professor and world-renowned author, discusses how vulnerability, courage and shame help shape self-awareness.[8] She says that what differentiates us as a social species is the need to be seen, known and loved, as well as the need to see and love others.

I have shared with you examples of three people who harnessed self-awareness not only in their personal lives but also in their professional practice. These individuals are clear about who they are and what they represent. They are also clear about the impact they have on others. Such self-awareness has a positive impact on workplace relationships and productivity.

What can you do to build your self-awareness?

Engaging in activities that focus on ourselves builds self-awareness. It's not hard to see that self-awareness develops gradually. Nevertheless, self-reflection helps us to recognise what we know and don't know about ourselves and how this impacts our interactions with others. The reflection process is a spiral of learning cycles, a repeated pattern of learning. Through reflection, we can draw conclusions about how we need to change our behaviour. That leads to more cycles of reflection and action to keep growing and developing our skills.

I want to highlight the importance of the reflection process. To do it well, we must be clear about the story that we tell ourselves. Sometimes we're so focused on wanting to be perceived in a particular way that we're not truthful of the facts. Here are four specific learning processes to develop self-awareness that explain what I mean.[9]

1. **Biases in self-perception** – Healthy self-awareness can be hindered by our own biases in self-perception. We may hold ourselves back by self-sabotaging, avoiding risks and having too much confidence. Programs for growth in both personal and professional aspects, along with quality coaching and guidance, can aid in gaining a better sense of self-awareness.

For example, you notice that a group of work colleagues regularly have drinks on Friday afternoons. Workers of the same age group are invited, but not others. When you ask why, those who organise the event assume that those outside the age group don't want to attend.

2. **Openness to learning** – We're willing to learn and adapt to different stages of life. When going through transitional periods, consistent and ongoing reflection is a great opportunity to actively participate in a strengthening process.

For example, a tech sprint takes place every Wednesday morning. All team members are required to share their work contribution to the project. Alex, Jasmine and Ravi take notes, ask questions and share insights from past product launches. The outcome is that by receiving feedback and contemplating new thoughts, individuals gain a better understanding of diverse perspectives.

When we're open to learning about the perspectives of self and others as well as being open to opportunities that come our way, we adopt a growth mindset. A growth mindset is advocated by Carol Dweck, a researcher in human motivation.[10] A growth mindset contributes to self-awareness, being open to growth of self and understanding the space of others. So, to return to Alex, Jasmine and Ravi in the tech sprint, the team members are inspired to bring creative solutions to their own responsibilities.

3. **Adopt a growth mindset** – Knowing how to manage yourself is crucial to understanding who you are. A strong sense of who you are (identity) and what you can do (efficacy) can help you deal with unpleasant situations more effectively. Mitigating emotions through coaching and mentoring goes a long way in handling difficult-to-hear feedback.

4. **Engage in regular self-reflection** – Take the time to reflect daily, journal, take long walks, or find whatever works for you to centre yourself.

Let's explore a scenario where feedback is delivered to someone with a growth mindset:

Scenario: Project Presentation

Context
- Alex, a junior software developer, recently completed a challenging project.
- The project involved complex coding, tight deadlines and collaboration with a cross-functional team.

Feedback Session
1. Positive Start

- Manager (M): 'Alex, I appreciate your hard work on the project. You demonstrated resilience and creativity.'
- Alex (A): 'Thank you. I learned a lot during this process.'

2. Constructive Feedback

    - M: 'However, there were areas for improvement.'
    - A: 'Go ahead.'

3. Specific Feedback

    - M: 'Your code quality was strong overall, but there were instances where comments were missing or unclear.'
    - A: 'I see. I'll work on that.'

4. Challenging Aspect

    - M: 'The presentation, though, was a challenge.'
    - A: 'How so?'

5. Honest Assessment

    - M: 'Your nerves affected your delivery. You stumbled over key points.'
    - A: 'I appreciate the honesty.'

6. Growth Mindset Response
    - A: 'I'll practice more and seek feedback. I want to improve my presentation skills.'

Result
    - Alex embraces the feedback, recognising it as an opportunity for growth.
    - The growth mindset allows for continuous learning and development.

• • •

Chapter 1: Takeaways

As we approach the end of this first chapter, it is clear that understanding the self is essential if we are to show up in a way that honours dignity, exemplifies integrity, and values relationships. Self-Awareness Matters!

At the beginning of this chapter, I introduced you to the story of the Horse and the Rider. The Horse, with its heart of fire, reminds us of our humanity—the beauty of feeling deeply. The Rider, with its cool intellect, keeps us on course. We must understand how we show up to navigate life's twists and turns. Are we leaning too heavily on the Horse's emotional force? Or are we ignoring its wisdom? Awareness bridges the gap. It lets us honour both travellers—the wild, passionate Horse and the thoughtful, strategic Rider.

So, my fellow travellers, let's ride together. Let's find that delicate equilibrium where emotion and reason dance—a symphony of self-awareness. And as we journey, let's remember that understanding ourselves helps us understand others.

There are seven key takeaways from this chapter.

1. **Definition of self** – self is a complex concept influenced by social interactions and personal connections.
2. **Consider the dynamic between three aspects of self-awareness** – self-evaluation, the process of learning about self, and intentionally and actively seeking moments of awareness.

3. **Intrapersonal and interpersonal awareness** – understanding our thoughts and how they impact others is key for both personal and professional development.
4. **Internal and external self-awareness** – internal self-awareness is achieved by understanding our values, beliefs, strengths and areas for improvement. External self-awareness means being aware of how others perceive us.
5. **Introspection and self-awareness** – engaging in the reflection process is important for us to understand the *why* of our actions.
6. **Impact of self-awareness** – the way we see ourselves and how we turn up for ourselves and others can greatly influence our ability to connect with others, manage our emotions and engage in a process of continuous self-improvement.
7. **Self-awareness** – understanding self – is essential to showing up in a way that honours dignity, exemplifies integrity, and values relationships. To be self-aware is to ...
    - Be you with *integrity*
    - Be you with *skill*
    - Be you with *courage*

Chapter Two

Values

• • •

The Tortoise and the Hare

A well-known Aesop fable describes the journey of a tortoise and a hare to a finish line. The tortoise chooses to partake in the race in a slow, methodical way, which aligns with its values of appreciating the journey and not the end. However, the hare values a challenge very differently. For the hare, it's all about winning and getting to the end first. For this reason, the hare runs fast – but that is its

weakness. You see, the hare has to stop and rest, allowing the tortoise to pass the hare and arrive at the finish line first. The story is timeless. However, it brings to the fore two key values: patience and perseverance.

• • •

What are values?

In Chapter 1, we focused on self-awareness and how this impacts the way we turn up for ourselves and others. Our values are determined by what we deem to be important, and they can affect how well we understand ourselves, or self-awareness. Sarah Monk, a clinical psychologist, says that values serve as a moral and ethical compass for our behaviour, a framework for quality decision-making and a yardstick for setting goals.[11] Values underpin our social interactions and our psychological safety, and ultimately are essential for living a quality life.

The following table of values is by no means exhaustive:

Honesty	Compassion	Integrity	Patience
Commitment	Generosity	Clarity	Achievement
Perseverance	Appreciation	Beauty	Adaptability
Accountability	Communication	Kindness	Humour

Values

Researchers tell us that values define individuals and cultures. Personal values are aligned with individuals and link to the goals, motivations and principles by which they live their lives. These values influence behaviour, cognition and perceptions. Culture impacts personal values because 'values are socially desirable'.[12] When we identify with a particular group, we share values and beliefs, which, in turn, help us justify choices or make judgements.

Although there's a great deal of theory outlining what values are and what they're not, three aspects of values are common. The first links values to the establishment of goals. In this context, values serve as drivers that guide behaviours necessary to meet important goals. The second common aspect refers to motivational values. These values become the linchpin for specific goals, such as choosing a profession or sport. Using a professional cricketer as an example, the value or prestige of the professional sportsperson determines the discipline required to achieve by following a commitment to training and appropriate behaviours. The third common aspect refers to personal value, which is aligned with hierarchical value. In other words, when a value holds more sway, a greater amount of energy and concentration are directed towards attaining it.

Public health campaigns and advertisers exploit the power of motivational values on individuals and populations. Public health promotions appeal to people's motivations by pointing out that if they choose a certain health behaviour (or turn away from an unhealthy behaviour) they will gain, achieve or benefit in a way that's aligned with their underlying values. Advertising does the same thing. Advertisers don't sell beverages (soft drinks, alcohol) or household goods or holidays; the consumer is not sold a product but rather a lifestyle or a pathway to a motivating value, impulse or aspiration – 'Buy this and you get that'.

The adoption of values may be influenced by how we are reared, the environment that surrounds us (including the media), workplace culture and social networks. For example, let's discuss the value of commitment. If we continue with the example of the professional cricketer, commitment includes a training regime that requires a strict schedule, a specific energy-based diet and nutrients, and a lifestyle that's conducive to supporting long hours of training. The cricketer understands that their goal will be achieved with the values of dedication, commitment and perseverance.

Alternatively, consider a freelancer who values and chooses flexibility in projects and clients instead of a long-term commitment with an employer. The freelancer chooses to work on different projects at various times, which requires varied knowledge, skills and understandings. For freelancers, adaptation to new situations and learning new skills shape their commitment to fulfilling set tasks.

The examples of the professional sportsperson and the freelancer illustrate commitment but notice how the value attached to their understanding and application of commitment is different. Values mean different things to different people.

Consider the following questions:

- If you could select a career without concern for money, what would it be? Why?

- What stories inspire you or annoy you when watching the evening news? Why?

- Can you recall key times in your life when you were happiest? Why? What was happening to you at those times?

- Think about a time when you faced an ethical dilemma either personally or professionally. How did you handle it?

- How do you work with people who challenge you?

Workplace values

In Chapter 1, we read about the importance of self-awareness to three successful businesspeople: Satya Nadella, Arianna Huffington and Brené Brown. For these individuals, the value of self-awareness enabled them to improve their understanding of themselves and those around them, bolster their confidence and self-assurance, and prioritise their own self-care or wellbeing.

Those three successful businesspeople led themselves and their respective organisations with three concepts I've already introduced: integrity, skill and courage.

How is your workplace impacted when you …

- Be you with *integrity*
- Be you with *skill*
- Be you with *courage*

Core values in the workplace

Work is an essential aspect of human activity. It provides income, the means for survival, and nurtures our ethical, moral, social, emotional, psychological and spiritual needs.

One of the challenges is making sure that core values become ingrained in a system that respects not only ourselves but also the dignity of others because they're essential for a healthy workplace, as emphasised by Michel Guillemin and Robin Nicholas.[13] Their research into the notion of an alignment of personal values with the organisation shows that 'core values at work must support the individual'. Core values form the base from which an organisation's culture grows.

Without this alignment, there's a disconnect that can have catastrophic consequences. Individuals whose values align with their workplace tend to be productive and engaged and are, overall, satisfied with their values.

What are your personal values and how do they align with those of your workplace?

The workplace plays a critical role in supporting the core values of employees because an individual's core values are significant in their personal and professional lives. Jack Phillips and Lisa Edwards help us to understand the idea of employee engagement or commitment to an organisation.[14] Core values impact commitment to an organisation or how you turn up for work and determine the degree to which you're so committed to an organisation that you'll invest extra effort to get the job done.

Phillips and Edwards identified two types of commitment: rational and emotional. A rational commitment to the workplace involves dedicating your energy, time, knowledge, skills and understanding towards achieving common workplace goals. Emotional commitment is drawn from core values that may include dignity and respect. When challenges arise, the emotional commitment guides the rational thought process. In fact, Phillips and Edwards have noted that emotional core values are four times more valuable than rational commitment within the workplace.

How do you respond to challenges in the workplace?

How do your values link to your motivation at work?

It's possible to classify motivation into external and internal dimensions.[15] The external dimension often aligns with the role and workplace conditions that exist outside an individual; they're usually short-lived. An individual's core values, however, drive internal motivations. Internal values are connected to belief systems that have grown over time and drive motivations for achieving goals.

The message in all of this is that positive strong emotions can drive incredible commitment and motivation in the workplace. On the other hand – employers beware! – employees' workplace commitment and motivation suffer if they don't feel heard or seen.

We know that although different organisations have different principles and values, their 'principles and values are the basis of making and keeping promises to employees and customers'.[16] For example, The Wesfarmers Group is an Australian corporation that provides services and resources to Western Australian farmers. Their four values are integrity, openness, accountability and entrepreneurial spirit. Ikea, a Swedish multinational corporation, provides furniture, appliances, home goods and services. It has eight values: togetherness, caring for people and the planet, cost-consciousness, simplicity, renew and improve, different with meaning, give and take responsibility, and lead by example.

Why do values matter in an organisation? Patrick Lencioni argues we should make our values mean something[17], and highlights values as the cornerstone for making quality decisions and nurturing workplace culture. It's a leader's role to make company values a lived experience for employees. A correct alignment of values for an organisation and its employees creates a mutually reciprocal context, ongoing connections and strategic support.

If we consider values as non-negotiable belief systems that matter to us, then core values are unalterable beliefs that remain constant regardless of what comes our way. Brent Gleeson, a Forbes contributor, defines core values as the 'guiding light that bonds a team with the same sense of purpose for achieving common goals'.[18] It stands to reason that if core values are deeply ingrained within an organisation then the resulting principles will heavily impact organisational culture and shape its teams. We're all familiar with LinkedIn. The company's core values are trust and care, innovation and valuing the workforce. Spotify's core values include innovation, sincerity and playfulness. Those core values, although different, declare the principles by which the respective companies intend to operate.

Let's look at the values of well-known people. You may be familiar with Martin Luther King Jr.'s 'I Have a Dream' speech, which emphasises the values of equality, justice and freedom. Martin Luther King was committed to a diverse USA that honoured everyone's dignity and where people felt they could belong. Satya Nadella, CEO of Microsoft, lives and breathes the value of empathy, inclusion and growth.[19] Satya's desire to understand and connect with all stakeholders influences the decisions and products made by the company. Similarly, the CEO of Apple, Tim Cook, has core values that emphatically endorse environmental responsibility and using ethical supply chains. Such core values become lived experiences for stakeholders through the introduction of renewable energy sources in the manufacturing of Apple's products, and the implementation of a closed-loop supply chain, which means Apple products are recycled as much as possible with a commitment to a net-zero climate impact by 2030.

It's fair to say, then, that the unique values of individuals and groups are the basis for their success in achieving what they consider important and significant.

• • •

Chapter 2: Takeaways

At the beginning of this chapter, we talked about the different values shared by the tortoise and the hare. We learnt there are varied approaches to attaining a goal. For the tortoise, it was slow and steady. For the hare, it was about the win. What stands out, however, is the values that we have and how we use those values to make quality decisions in the workplace.

There are seven key takeaways from this chapter.

1. **Definition and importance of values** – values are moral frames that guide our words and actions. They play a critical role in goal setting and in making appropriate decisions.

2. Values are **motivational drivers** that underpin goal setting.

3. **Aligned personal and organisational values** increase productivity and meet mutually reciprocal goals.

4. Values **differ** in various contexts.

5. **Values impact motivation.** Goals driven by internal motivation are of greater value than those externally driven.

6. Core values **drive influential leaders**. Their values guide their decisions and actions.

7. Your core values **empower** you to …
    - Be you with *integrity*
    - Be you with *skill*
    - Be you with *courage*

Chapter Three

Emotional Intelligence

• • •

The Lion and the Donkey

Another Aesop story brings to light the importance of emotional intelligence. As the lion walks in the forest, he's insulted by a donkey. The lion is triggered by the comment but stays in control of his emotions and continues on the journey without saying a word to the donkey.

• • •

Therein lies our introduction to this chapter – how emotional intelligence can help us to not only be more self-aware but live our values in a way that honours ourselves and others.

Have you ever had a conversation with someone and thought, *Why did I respond so defensively?* Or *Why do I feel so fearful about having the meeting with Jim?* Or *I notice that Anna hides at work when we meet with the board. Why does she do that?*

In the book, *It's All About IT!* I spent some time talking about the amygdala and its role in protecting the human body. If you've not yet had a chance to read the book, here's a quick overview of the amygdala and its impact on emotional intelligence.

The amygdala is an almond-shaped structure located in the middle part of the brain that is called the Limbic System.

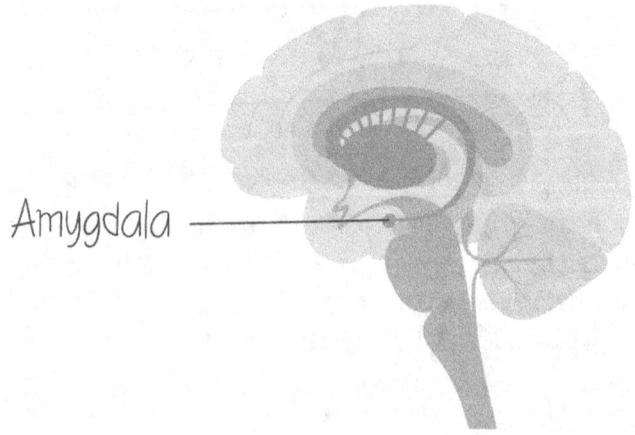

It's responsible for the fight, flight and freeze responses that occur when the body senses danger. The danger can be physical, emotional or psychological. The amygdala collates data through the senses to determine our protective actions. For example, if an out-of-control car crosses our path, we automatically react. The priority of the amygdala is to remove us from harm's way.

Or when we are caring for an ill child, our heightened stress levels might cause us to struggle to understand the information a health professional is sharing.

The action of the amygdala is comparable to a superhero swooping in to help but sometimes with unanticipated results. For example, when a coworker yells at us, we might feel anxious, fearful or even angry. These emotional reactions can be the cause of ongoing stress and worry.

To help us benefit from a partnership with the amygdala, we need to recognise our emotions, how they're triggered and what we can do to consciously protect ourselves.

What are emotions?

Various theories offer different perspectives about emotions, which are complex and multifaceted. The Schachter-Singer theory (1962) states that emotion is about the cognitive and physical response to a situation. In other words, an individual's response to a situation is shaped by their perception of the surrounding environment. For instance, imagine walking in an unlit car park at night and two unknown men dressed in dark clothes and wearing balaclavas appear. Your perception of that environment is likely to increase your heart rate and prompt an instinctive reaction, which might be to run or something else.

Similarly, Keltner and Gross[20] argue that emotions arise in response to physical and social challenges. Four factors help us to understand emotions: behaviour, feelings, thoughts and physiology. Behaviour encompasses action and communication, and experiences are linked to feelings. Experiences lead to thoughts, and thoughts can lead to physiological changes. All four factors have the potential to change following a specific event, whether it happens internally or externally.

What is emotional intelligence?

If emotions are about how we respond to situations, emotional intelligence is a profound concept that invites us to learn and manage our emotions with skill. Understanding and effectively engaging in the use of emotional intelligence means that we are able to self-regulate, communicate more effectively and develop quality relationships especially in the work place. Emotional intelligence, as defined by Stein and Book[21], 'is the ability to perceive emotions, to access and generate emotions to assist thought, to understand emotions and emotional meanings, and to reflectively regulate emotions in ways that promote emotional and intellectual growth'. That definition underscores the importance of emotions in our cognitive processes and personal development.

The Reuven Bar-On model, named after the psychologist who pioneered research into emotional intelligence, measures Emotional Intelligence

Quotient (EQ-i), which is widely used by individuals and organisations to learn and further develop their emotional intelligence.

The model uses norm-referenced questions to determine emotional intelligence scores in five areas relating to emotionally and socially intelligent behaviour.

1. Self-perception – understanding and appreciating one's own emotions.

2. Self-expression – effectively expressing emotions and communicating feelings.

3. Interpersonal skills – building and maintaining healthy relationships through quality social communication skills.

4. Decision-making – using emotional intelligence to make quality decisions.

5. Stress management – adaptively managing stress.

This framework of measures guides an assessment of emotional intelligence and ways to improve it. By being aware of how we turn up (our behaviour and communication) we can improve our ability to connect with others. This can lead to positive relationships and better decision-making through problem-solving and reality testing. Important strategies for developing emotional intelligence are managing stress through understanding your limits, being open to new ideas and possibilities, and staying flexible and adaptable.

How to review, renew and regenerate emotional intelligence in the workplace

In using these strategies, we're reinforcing four key points.

1. **Become aware of negative thought patterns.** For some of us, the burden of past experiences makes us feel unworthy or conditions us to believe that perfection is necessary for validation.

   For instance, Jane spends long hours at work, often leaving very late in the evening. It is important to her that every task is completed with great precision. She's always tired and has lost her desire to keep working.

   Although striving for excellence is important, it's equally vital to accept that perfection isn't always attainable. Instead of being overly critical of ourselves, we should set realistic goals with achievable time frames, and complete tasks effectively without undue stress.

2. **The power of pause.** Taking a moment to pause and reflect on a situation can be incredibly powerful.

John, a production manager, believes there's no time to reflect on his role. From the time he starts work at 5:00 am until he leaves at 7:00 pm, only to return home to a young family, he feels spent. He's noticed that in addition to feeling tired, he's not able to effectively forward plan at work.

The power to pause invites us to gather our thoughts, assess situations and how we feel about them, and develop a plan to achieve our goals. Take the time to reflect on the situation. Establish a plan that will guide you to achieve the relevant outcomes.

3. **An emotional intelligence partner.** A trusted person can be a valuable support and give perspective when we share our feelings. However, we should establish very clear boundaries and expectations to ensure there's a mutual understanding. Having the ability to express emotions is important for building healthy relationships in a workplace.

Anita and Andrew have been working together as supervisors on a remote mine site for five years. Given their location, it's not always possible to connect with their families to share insights or challenges. Anita and Andrew have established clear boundaries about trust, confidentiality and mutual reciprocity as part of their work relationship. They're both mindful of how they turn up and how others see them turn up. Their clear boundaries enable them to share the challenges of the day without fear of breaches.

4. **Professional learning.** Engaging in professional learning provides valuable insights and techniques to enhance our EI. According to the World Economic Forum, emotional intelligence is among the 10 most in-demand skills and is anticipated to be so for a long time to come. In fact, McKinsey research predicts the demand for emotional intelligence will grow by 26 percent by 2030.[22] Interestingly, although emotional intelligence is regarded as a significant factor in the workplace, only 42 percent of companies provide training to grow employees in emotional intelligence, according to the Niagara Institute.[23]

Learning about and being trained in emotional intelligence helps us recognise our thought patterns, seek support and guidance from trusted individuals, and develop techniques to manage workplace stress and make better decisions.

Why is emotional intelligence so important for leaders in workplaces?

Leaders are more and more accountable for their impact on teams and organisations. Research by Lee Hecht and colleagues[24] revealed that over half (57 percent) of the 500 managers they interviewed believed that emotional intelligence was a common trait among members of high-performing teams. The study also highlighted that emotional intelligence is crucial for effective leadership, particularly in areas such as change management (44 percent), communicating with staff on personal matters (37 percent) and providing quality feedback (31 percent).

Leadership can significantly influence the success or failure of teams and organisations. A study of 155,000 leaders found just 22 percent demonstrated strong emotional intelligence.[25] That same study identified a strong correlation between a leader's self-awareness and the overall climate of their team. Effective and functional leaders have emotional self-awareness, empathy, quality interpersonal relationships, quality decision-making skills and an optimistic approach to their work.[26]

The importance of emotional intelligence and the tragic consequences of the absence of emotional intelligence in leadership was highlighted in the findings of an Australian Royal Commission into the causes of 'an epidemic' of suicide among the Australian Defence Force's members and veterans.[27] A commission recommendation was for defence personnel to be assessed for emotional intelligence when being considered for promotion and leadership. The recommendation cited the following indicators used by the defence force of the United Kingdom when assessing the emotional intelligence of potential leaders: leadership, teamwork and collaboration, communication and influence, physical and mental resilience, values and standards, respect for others, integrity and discipline.

With the insights into self-awareness (Chapter 1), values (Chapter 2), and understanding our emotions (in this chapter), we have gained a better understanding of how we turn up for ourselves and others.

Consider some of these scenarios

1. *Jason arrives at work a bit flustered and late. His morning had been a whirlwind, with little Molly adamantly refusing to wear her school uniform. He loves his daughter, but mornings are often a battleground, leaving him feeling drained before the day even begins. As he finally sits down at his desk, the weight of the morning chaos still lingers.*

   In the psychologically unsafe environment of his workplace, Jason is grappling with mixed emotions: frustration from the morning's struggle with Molly, guilt for being late to work and anxiety about potential repercussions in the office. He has a sense of helplessness, caught between love for his daughter and the demands of his job. The emotional turmoil challenges Jason's ability to focus and perform effectively, highlighting the importance of a supportive and understanding work environment.

How does Jason turn up for his daughter, employer and fellow employees? In what ways could his lateness and exhaustion impact his work? What can Jason do to grow his emotional intelligence?

2. *Winona, the compassionate manager of a pastoral care team, leads a diverse group of 12 individuals, each with unique skills and strengths. She's deeply attuned to her team's heavy workloads and the overwhelming stress they face. Among her staff, two have particularly short tempers, requiring her to carefully navigate their moods. Three others seem disengaged, two work tirelessly, and the remaining members are just coasting along.*

Winona herself feels a growing frustration. The constant need to placate the more challenging staff members to prevent outbursts is draining. She finds herself in a delicate balancing act, striving to maintain harmony and productivity within her team. Despite the challenges, Winona's commitment to her team's wellbeing remains unwavering as she continues to seek ways to support and motivate each member with the hope of fostering a more cohesive and resilient team environment. Winona is tired and in need of advice. She wonders how to better manage her team's dynamics and her stress. She wants strategies to create a more balanced and supportive workplace for everyone.

How does Winona's exhaustion define how she turns up for work? Which aspect of the Reuven Bar-On model would she need to explore more to mitigate her workplace challenges?

3. *John, the dedicated Head of Marketing at Jorge Enterprises, genuinely loves his job. His passion for his work is evident in every campaign he oversees and every strategy he develops. However, John struggles with having courageous conversations. The last time he attempted one, his hands trembled so much that some of his coffee spilled, and his voice became shaky, leaving him feeling terrible. His vulnerability is noticed by those he needs to speak with; they're often aware of his discomfort and lack of confidence during these interactions.*

   Although highly skilled in his profession, this obstacle is currently affecting John's exceptional performance. John yearns to communicate more effectively and to express his thoughts and concerns without the physical manifestations of his anxiety. He dreams of a day when he can hold these conversations with the same confidence and clarity he brings to his marketing strategies. Until then, he continues to navigate this personal hurdle, hoping to find the strength and support he needs to overcome it.

   How can John grow his emotional intelligence to mitigate courageous conversations?

• • •

Chapter 3: Takeaways

We began this chapter with Aesop's fable about the lion and the donkey. The lion didn't react to the thoughtless comment made by the donkey. In this case, he opted not to respond. In emotional intelligence terms, the lion was very clear about who he was and his choice of response to the donkey. To put it simply, emotional intelligence explains how we perceive, access and regulate our emotions in ways that cultivate quality responses to situations in our personal and professional lives.

There are five key takeaways from this chapter.

1. Emotional intelligence is **essential** for effective communication, relationship building, decision-making and stress management.
2. **Recognise emotional triggers** – the amygdala is responsible for triggering our emotions related to the flight, fright and freeze responses. Being able to manage our triggers helps us to better connect with others.
3. Emotional intelligence can be **developed** by self-regulation, self-management, interpersonal skills, stress management and learning opportunities.
4. Understanding emotional intelligence is **essential for everyone**, particularly those seeking a leadership position.
5. To effectively use emotional intelligence is to ...
   - Be you with *integrity*
   - Be you with *skill*
   - Be you with *courage*

Chapter Four

Resilience

• • •

The story of Nick Vujicic

Nick Vujicic was born with Tetra-Amelia syndrome, which left him without arms or legs. He faced immense challenges from a young age, including battling depression as he navigated the realities of life without limbs. Nick's story is a testament to resilience. He navigated the experiences of being a young boy wanting to climb trees and play games

and then engage in his adolescent years hanging out with his friends. He studied accounting and financial planning and has become one of the world's most renowned motivational speakers. Today, Nick is married and the father of four children. Despite ongoing challenges, Nick has inspired many through his remarkable resilience and commitment to living his best life despite the obstacles he has had to and continues to face. In this chapter, we will learn about resilience and how it shapes our presence in the workplace.

• • •

When you think of resilience, what word comes to mind? Perhaps you thought of terms such as tenacity, courage, commitment, determination, strength, transparency, reliability.

When you think of resilient people, who comes to mind?

- Malala Yousafzai (1997–present)
- Nelson Mandela (1918–2013)
- Helen Keller (1880–1968)
- Richard Branson (1950–present)
- Jacinda Ardern (1980–present)

These public figures are acknowledged for resilience in their respective contexts. Other individuals have shown great resilience in their own unique situations, whether they're public figures or people we know personally, such as parents, grandparents, siblings, friends or colleagues. Their experiences and wisdom can be just as valuable, if not more so, than the resilience we observe in well-known individuals in our community.

What is resilience?

For some, resilience involves leveraging strengths, whereas, for others, resilience encompasses gauging one's grit, passion and perseverance to complete tasks. You may have also heard that resilience was once about bouncing back from adversity. Bouncing back explains how people or organisations come back from a challenging situation. The notion is now challenged by researchers such as Brené Brown[28], who highlights personal or professional growth as a result of the upheaval that might cause people and organisations to bounce forward. What is clear from the literature on resilience is that it's a process that's not necessarily trait-driven but skill-developed to highlight positive adaptation to situations.[29]

Dr Nancy Bonfiglio-Pavisich

What is resilience in the workplace from an individual perspective?

In the workplace, resilience means being able to consistently handle tough situations and still get things done. For example, someone who stays calm under pressure despite challenging circumstances, or a team that overcomes a major project setback and still produces great work.

Silja Hartman and her colleagues identify two aspects of resilience in any workplace.[30] The first is experiencing adversity, which may consist of periods of great intensity, such as non-negotiable deadlines or degrees of isolation. The second is the capacity to positively adapt to such periods of adversity or intensity. The capacity to adapt is aligned with the coping strategies individuals use to bounce forward after hardships.

For example, researchers have identified individual risk and protective factors that determine the capacity of early career teachers to respond to hardship with resilience.[31] Individual risk factors include:

1. Mindset

2. Lack of confidence in self and seeking support

3. A disconnect between personal values and those of the organisation.

The individual risk factors can be mitigated by protective factors that, when implemented, can help early career teachers show their strength and ability to bounce forward from challenges. Protective factors are resources that include:

1. Self-efficacy, including the capacity to engage in regular reflection

2. Confidence and competence

3. Enhanced problem-solving skills.

The combined work of several researchers[32] makes it possible to categorise resilience into four specific areas. Resilience is experienced when these four areas operate in harmony with one another.

1. **Personal resources** – self-efficacy, social competence and confidence.

2. **Motivation** – sense of purpose and meaning, commitment, and professional goals.

3. **Emotions** – positive, bounce forward, not personalising decisions.

4. **Profession-related** – knowledge, leadership styles and social support.

Citrin and Weiss (2016) use the term grit to explore resilience. Mitigating adversity may look like the following:

1. **Embrace failure** – how we deal with failure determines our degree of resilience. Learning from the errors we have made and focusing on them objectively rather than taking them personally helps to build resilience.

2. **Be persistent** – this involves being committed to the task despite the challenges that arise. The researchers believe that time and focus underpin persistence. The more time we have, the more we can mitigate challenges. Unfortunately, this is not always the way.

3. **Grow passion** – developing a passion to do and be better also supports concepts aligned with resilience.

4. **A growth mindset** – being open to possibilities, rethinking how things are done, and reviewing the lens through which we see things supports key growth in resilience.

Resilience

Mitigate Adversity

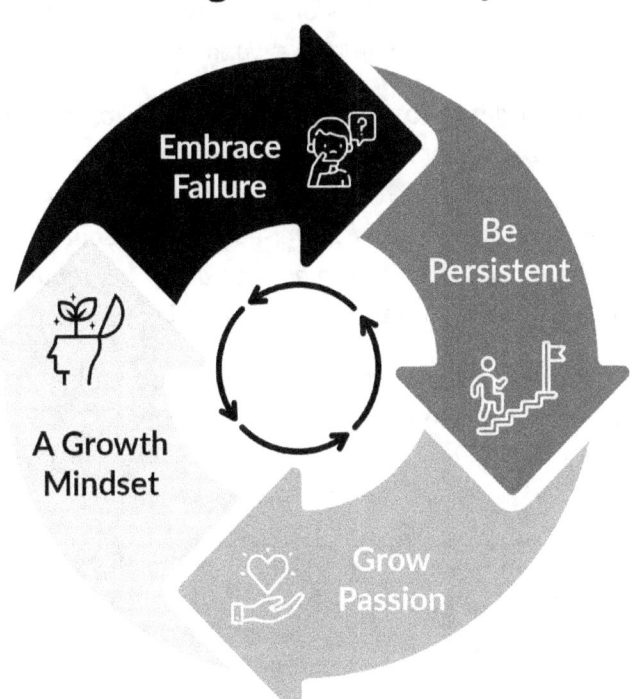

Take the time to think about your current position in these four categories. In your workplace, how do things seem, feel and sound to you? What actions can you take to improve or reduce your resilience at work?

Consider the following vignette

Jan, a supervisor for ABC Limited, has been in mining for 10 years, working a roster of two weeks off and two weeks on. She's been asked to take on another leadership role for a short period, which would mean a roster change to three weeks on and two weeks off. Jan loves her team of 10 people and is very comfortable working alongside them.

In addition to the disruption to her roster, Jan is worried about not having the necessary skills to complete the job on time and feels anxious about meeting the deadlines despite being promised all the resources that will be required. Jan is also anxious about her reputation and is concerned that the new team will not like her.

Which of the four areas discussed earlier could Jan explore further to grow her resilience?

What is resilience in the workplace from a team perspective?

The concept of a resilient workplace team is relatively new. However, a resilient workplace team requires collective efficacy, which is the shared belief in a team's ability to achieve its goals and to be creative. As with individual resilience, resilient workplace teams have contextual risks and protective factors.

Examples of risk factors that may get in the way of a team's resilience may consist of:

1. The team's attitude to the team's vision, mission, values, and goals.

2. The interpersonal processes may not foster open, transparent communication.

3. The structural aspects of the team roles that may get in the way of the collective work being achieved.

Examples of protective factors that support a team's resilience may include:

1. High-level flexibility and quality problem-solving and decision-making.

2. Positive team behaviours reflective of mutually respectful attitudes about colleagues and the organisation.

3. Collective efficacy and drive to achieve the team's targets despite challenges.

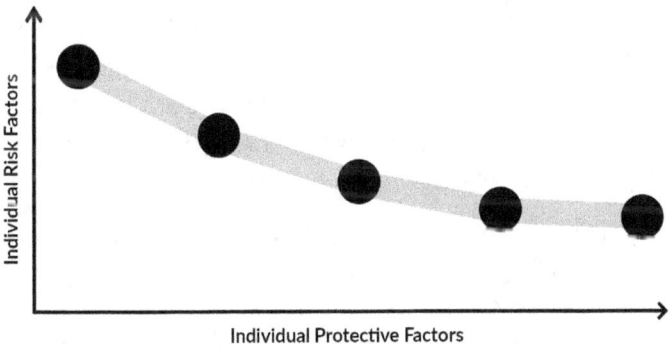

What do you think your Risk and Protective Factor Graph looks like?

Consider the following vignette about collective resilience

The production team has been working together for the last 18 months. The team consists of a production team manager and eight staff members. Five team members are full-time and three are part-time. Two of the five full-time members – who have been with the organisation for six years – have a fixed mindset about how tasks should be completed. The other team members have been with the organisation for three and four years. They have a growth mindset and they value opportunities to think outside the square and adopt new approaches to old problems.

The team manager has had one-on-one conversations with all team members. He's learnt that the two team members with fixed mindsets journeyed through a turbulent economic and financial time with the organisation in the first year of their appointment. Although the production team is currently experiencing challenges, the trauma of their experience has made them less confident in taking risks to address those challenges. That explains why they are reticent.

What are your thoughts about your team's resilience in the workplace?

What do you believe needs to happen to grow the team?

What role does the production team manager have in this space?

• • •

Chapter 4: Takeaways

We began this chapter recognising Nick Vujicic's resilience. Given that 'there are only 24 hours, 1440 minutes or 86,400 seconds in a day'[33], I invite you to consider the choices you can make about how you turn up for yourself and others with resilience at work. Being resilient requires you to be aware of your risk factors and how you might implement protective factors to address them.

There are five key takeaways from this chapter.

1. Resilience is a **dynamic process** that leverages strengths, passion and positive mindsets to overcome adversity.

2. Individual risk and protective factors are **critical to developing resilience**. Individual risk factors include: lack of confidence and lack of support. Protective factors include: support systems, problem-solving skills and a positive mindset.

3. There are **four classifications of resilience:** personal resources, motivation, emotion and profession-related factors.

4. **Examples** of resilient public figures are Malala Yousafzai, Nelson Mandela, Helen Keller, Richard Branson and Jacinda Ardern.

5. To practice resilience is to ...
    - Be you with *integrity*
    - Be you with *skill*
    - Be you with *courage*

PART 2

How Do Others See You Turn Up?

Part 2 encourages you to reflect on how you turn up for others in terms of:

- Engagement and motivation
- Accountability
- Quality decision-making
- Leadership.

How do others see you turn up?

This is a profound question that often sparks introspection. In my workshops, I've noticed it can be a challenge to formulate a comprehensive answer. Why? Perhaps it's because many of us are so engrossed in our daily tasks that we rarely pause to consider the question. We're focused on the job at hand, the next deadline or the next meeting.

When I invite people to think deeply about that question, the answers tend to be around key character traits. For some, we must turn up as reliable. Others cite being consistent in decision-making or that being dependable when it counts is a precursor to establishing and maintaining a basis of trust. Participants have deemed trust to be an essential component of a workplace relationship. Limited goodwill exists if a leader, colleague or client is untrustworthy.

Others say that being authentic in our words and actions is crucial. It's how we show up for others. A heightened amygdala (responsible for the flight, fright and freeze responses) will be activated when we don't feel psychologically safe around people. It's crucial to create a safe and authentic environment in our professional interactions.

Other qualities shared by workshop participants for the way we show up for others are humility, positivity and empathy. Humility is regarded as self-awareness and understanding of others. Positivity is linked to having a positive mindset and conquering challenges with grit and tenacity. Empathy is often referred to as understanding the thoughts, words and actions of others instead of being judgemental. Such qualities not only empower us but also enrich our professional relationships.

When I ask participants to name renowned people who turn up or turned up exceptionally well for others, Jacinda Ardern, Richard Branson and Barack Obama are among the names offered. Participants share insights such as these about those people.

Jacinda Ardern was the prime minister of New Zealand from 2017 to 2023. Although her political legacy has been subject to scrutiny and criticism, Ardern's personal legacy is of a compassionate and empathetic politician whose humanity was widely admired as she managed a series of crises during her term of office. She won international acclaim for her response to the 2019 Christchurch mosque massacre of 51 Muslims by a gunman. She met with the families of those who had lost loved ones, spoke with community leaders, and communicated with impact in speeches that focused on equality and inclusion. Politics aside, Arden turned up as a kind and emotionally intelligent leader.

In 2017, Priyansha Mistry wrote an article in the online HR Digest about Richard Branson.[34] The article, 'Clients do not come first. Employees come first', noted that Branson turns up by practising what he preaches. His openly communicated and lived philosophy is that employees are the business. He's a leader who supports a common purpose and vision in every way, shape and form. Richard Branson encourages employees to have a sense of ownership. He believes this leads to a culture of willing growth and development that benefits productivity and outcomes.

As the first African American president in the White House, Barack Obama is often referred to as someone who was and continues to be a compassionate individual whose empathetic and impassioned approach is embodied by his engagement with people at the grassroots level. For example, during his presidency, Obama attended the funeral of Reverend Clementa Pinckney, who was killed in the Charleston Church shooting that took place in 2015. During the funeral service, Obama shared a eulogy and sang 'Amazing Grace' with the congregation.

These examples typify people who foster deep connections with others by providing support, encouragement and commitment in a psychologically safe environment. These people who engage and motivate others exude leadership to guide quality decision-making. The chapters in this section ask you to consider how the qualities mentioned can help you to turn up for others.

Chapter Five

Engagement at Work

• • •

The North Wind and the Sun

The North Wind and the Sun is another of Aesop's fables that suggests how we treat others, leading to their engagement with us. In this story, the sun and the wind have a quarrel about which of them is stronger. They agree that the strongest would be the one to remove the cloak from a passing traveller. No matter how hard the wind blew, the traveller pulled the cloak tightly around himself.

The sun, waiting patiently, decided to shine. As the sun's rays warmed the traveller, he removed his cloak.

• • •

The lesson is that engagement is better than force. When applied to the workplace, our engagement is guided by considering underlying motivations or reasons for an employee's or colleague's behaviour. In my first book, *It's All About IT! – A guide to better communication and mastering conversation skills in the workplace*, I discussed Simon Sinek's insights on understanding the *why* behind actions. By understanding and communicating effectively, and with personal humility and professional will, we can better grasp our own purposes and those of others. Jim Collins, a leadership author and speaker, emphasises how better performance is achieved by improving working conditions: 'Make work better for people and people work better for you'.

If we are to engage with others and be better able to understand them, we need to start with respect. I define respect as 'honouring the dignity of the human person'. Engaging with respect and honouring others' dignity requires the skills of self-awareness (Chapter 1), clarity about our values (Chapter 2), and emotional intelligence (Chapter 3).

What is engagement?

Engagement is all about having a purpose, a sense of belonging and a commitment to a cause, event or place. The difference between engagement and motivation is that motivation requires drive or energy to commit to being engaged. What's common to engagement and motivation is self-determination theory (SDT), which explains the natural and intrinsic factors that lead to behaviour.[35]

What is employee/colleague engagement?

There are no formal definitions of employee engagement so to be clear, I'm using the terms 'employee' and 'colleague' in the same context of employee engagement.

According to Julia Bogyo[36], employee engagement characterises the relationship between organisations and employees, which influences the extent to which employees engage with their organisation and its strategies and goals. Three psychological conditions are necessary for engagement: psychological meaningfulness (deriving value and respect from work), psychological safety (feeling safe to learn, contribute, take risks and challenge the status quo) and psychological availability (ensuring that people aren't burned out or overly stressed).[37]

A Gallup meta-analysis study in 2020 sought to explore how well employee engagement predicted performance outcomes.[38] The research included 276 organisations from 54 industries across 96 countries. The findings provided significant validation of the correlation between engagement and workplace performance. The results showed a significant correlation – being engaged in your work relates to how well you perform on the job.

Take the time to read the stories below. They come from participants in my workshops who have given me permission to share their experiences about situations that impacted their workplace engagement. Of course, for privacy reasons names and other details have been changed.

Sarah

In a bustling office, Sarah felt increasingly isolated. Her once-vibrant team had grown distant, and collaboration dwindled as meetings became mere formalities. She tried to engage but her ideas were often overlooked, causing her to feel undervalued and disconnected. The lack of camaraderie weighed heavily, affecting Sarah's motivation and productivity. It wasn't just about the work; the sense of belonging had faded away, leaving her yearning for the days when teamwork felt like a shared adventure.

James

James, a talented graphic designer, found his creativity stifled under the constant scrutiny of his line manager. Every task, no matter how small, was micromanaged, leaving James feeling suffocated and doubting his abilities. The relentless oversight eroded his confidence. He became anxious and developed a sense of helplessness. The joy James once found in his work was replaced by dread and his mental health began to deteriorate. The office, once a place of inspiration, became a source of stress. Micromanagement had that impact on his wellbeing.

Emma

Emma, a dedicated project manager, consistently delivered exceptional results, but her ambitious colleague, Mark, often took credit for her ideas. During meetings, he subtly dismissed her contributions as he positioned himself as the driving force behind their team's success. Emma's frustration grew as her hard work went unrecognised, leading to feelings of inadequacy and resentment. The constant undermining not only affected her confidence but also strained her relationships with other colleagues. Despite the challenges, Emma remained resilient, determined to reclaim her voice and recognition.

What are your thoughts about the situations faced by Sarah, James and Emma? What can each of them do to address the situation? What role does their respective line manager have in helping them address the situation?

Employee/colleague engagement

We've already seen that engagement is about being part of an organisation, a common sense of purpose, belonging and commitment. It's important here to discuss a little about the motivations that enable us to stay engaged at work.

There are two types of motivations: intrinsic and extrinsic motivation.[39] Intrinsic motivation is about engaging in activities for personal interest or enjoyment, such as a person with a passion for learning more about cars; that curiosity stems from within. Extrinsic motivation drives the engagement of externally influenced activities. For example, your new CEO loves playing golf. You decide to learn to play golf and grow a connection with him. That external influence drives your interest in golf as a way to connect with your CEO; it's not driven by a personal desire to learn.

Motivation

Intrinsic Motivation
Internal reward
Choice
Enjoyable
Satisfying
Autonomy, Competence
and Relatedness

Extrinsic Motivation
External Reward
Money
Fame
Power
Avoid consequences

When our psychological needs are satisfied, we're more likely to be motivated and committed to our work. The more committed we are, the more value we provide the organisation. The benefits of being intrinsically motivated include being curious, working at optimal levels and collaborating with others.

The impact of employee engagement can be understood in three parts, as illustrated by the figure on page 72.[40] The first impact is rewards and recognition. The second is empowerment as our responsibilities and roles progress within the organisation. The third is better relationships with our respective line managers and organisational leaders.

Impact of Employee Engagement

Rewards & Recognition

Empowering Employees

Workplace Relationships

Rewards and recognition

When individuals are acknowledged for their work and given suitable rewards, there's a stronger connection between how engaged they are in their job, their overall performance and how satisfied they are in their role.

Rewards and recognition are part of the feedback process that impacts performance. Acknowledging the work of employees by validating their hard work and including them in quality decision-making makes them feel that their contributions are valued.

Examples of rewards and recognition include: [41]

1. Showcasing how the work contributes to the global community

2. Embedding recognition tools in the work to give instant feedback

3. Organising gift cards, raffles or email campaigns

4. Creating point systems that lead to achievement or performance being recognised

5. Providing meaningful recognition moments, e.g. monthly meetings

6. Telling stories in the long-held human tradition of sharing insights gained (good or bad) from experiences, to learn valuable lessons and define frames of reference.

Empowering employees

Employees are empowered when they're assured of autonomy, receive intrinsic rewards, and feel they have influence.[42] Employees are empowered knowing they're trusted by their leaders, given training and resources to do their jobs effectively and want to be given opportunities to work to their strengths in the workplace.

Factors that empower employees include:[43]

1. Being given opportunities for training, and opportunities to work to their strengths and take on other responsibilities such as leadership

2. Transparent communication in the workplace that is regular, transparent and delivered to meet the needs of all staff

3. Effective policies, practices, procedures and frameworks that ensure all stakeholders have clear expectations and boundaries for doing their jobs well

4. Creating a psychologically safe space for evidence-based feedback that motivates individuals to learn, contribute, take risks and challenge the status quo

5. Personal and professional goals that form part of ongoing conversations to support inclusivity and growth.

Building a bond between employees and leaders

The next chapter will expand on how employees and leaders can build healthy relationships. For the moment, note that the role of leaders in supporting the personal and professional growth of staff is essential to maintaining positive relationships.

We know that employee engagement is a byproduct of leadership by leaders who take the time to connect with employees, share their vision and mission, and communicate effectively about the organisation. Such leadership strengthens employee engagement by increasing the employees' commitment and motivation to the organisation. Similarly, when employers provide learning opportunities, quality resources and effective leadership, employees become more engaged with the policies and practices of the company. Getting this right ensures that the engagement of each individual contributes to the vitality, survivability and profitability of the organisation.[44]

• • •

Chapter 5: Takeaways

To return to Aesop's story about the wind and the sun, we learn that engagement is better than force. Employee engagement at work is achieved by engaging with people, taking time to get to know them and understanding what motivates them.

There are seven key takeaways from this chapter.

1. **Open communication** and **positive influence** create quality engagement in the workplace.

2. Engagement is **impacted by working conditions**. Feeling psychologically safe at work is essential for all stakeholders to work to their potential.

3. Engagement **starts with respect and dignity**, self-awareness, clear values, boundaries and expectations.

4. **Intrinsic and extrinsic motivation** support curiosity and performance.

5. **Empowerment** underpinned by a sense of belonging, commitment and purpose are essential aspects of engagement at work.

6. **Quality relationships** between leaders and the teams they lead fosters collegial and productive engagement.

7. To engage well in the workplace is to ...
    - Be you with *integrity*
    - Be you with *skill*
    - Be you with *courage*

Chapter Six

Accountability at Work

• • •

Everybody, Somebody,
Anybody and Nobody

This story is about four people named Everybody, Somebody, Anybody and Nobody. There was an important job to be done, and Everybody was asked to do it. Everybody was sure Somebody would do it. Anybody could have done it, but Nobody did it. Somebody got angry about that because it was Everybody's job. Everybody thought

Anybody could do it, but Nobody realised that Everybody wouldn't do it. And so, Everybody blamed Somebody when Nobody did what Anybody could have done.

• • •

This widely quoted story vividly illustrates the dire consequences of a lack of ownership, accountability and responsibility in the workplace. Let's delve into the crucial topic of accountability and its profound impact on the workplace.

What is accountability?

Accountability is recognising that other team members and general company performance depend on you. Accountable employees take responsibility for results and don't assume it's someone else's job. In an accountable workplace, everyone owns their behaviour and actions, which is the opposite of passing the buck, shifting responsibility or blaming someone else.

Two frames to accountability

Accountability is framed by the conditions that foster accountability and ownership, taking responsibility for tasks.

Frame One: Conditions that foster accountability

Accountability is framed by three conditions. The first is a supportive environment. A supportive environment depends on the respective workplace context. In a psychologically safe environment, leaders and managers make you feel that you're included at work, that you have the right to learn and contribute, and they will allow you to take reasonable risks and challenge the status quo. Here's an example.

Manager: 'Our team values open communication and collaboration. Please don't hesitate to reach out if you ever feel overwhelmed or need assistance. We have regular check-ins every Monday to discuss any challenges and provide support where needed. Additionally, we encourage you to take advantage of our professional development resources to help you grow in your role.'

Employee: 'Thank you! I appreciate the open-door policy and the emphasis on teamwork. I'll communicate any difficulties I encounter and participate actively in the check-ins. I'm also excited to explore the professional development opportunities to enhance my skills.'

The second condition that fosters accountability is clear expectations and open communication. With established boundaries of communication, we can be open, honest and accepting of others' ideas or ways of doing things. Clarity in expectations is a cornerstone of effective communication and accountability in the workplace that eliminates guesswork or making assumptions.

Employer: *'As part of your role, you must submit weekly progress reports by Friday afternoon at five o'clock. The reports should include updates on your current projects, challenges and plans for the upcoming week. This helps us stay aligned and address any issues promptly.'*

Employee: *'Understood. I will ensure that my progress reports are detailed and submitted on time every Friday. If I encounter any obstacles that might delay my report, I will inform you as soon as possible to discuss potential solutions.'*

The third condition for accountability is recognition and rewards. The celebration of achievements acknowledges excellent work, practice or behaviour.

There's a need for caution here: get to know people first and learn how they want to be acknowledged or rewarded. Sometimes there's a great difference between what you think is a celebration strategy and what someone else wants or needs.

For example, I was contacted by an executive IT team to work with them and their emerging leaders. At the first meeting with the executive, I asked, 'What would you say the entire IT team say you do well?' One team member indicated that when they celebrate the excellent work of staff, they align it with monthly birthday celebrations. They were so excited by this and thought their entire staff loved it. The story was very different when I met up with the emerging leaders. In fact, many didn't appreciate having their birthdays recognised, but they understood it was a social practice and went along with it. What offended them the most was that the executive team ran around an hour before the monthly birthday celebrations to find out whose work was worthy of recognition. People with the loudest or most popular voices were heard, resulting in the same people being recognised for a job well done. When I shared this with the executive team, they were shocked. Consequently, both groups worked together to design a celebratory process that both groups respected.

Frame Two: The ownership of accountability
When we talk about the ownership of accountability, we refer to actions and behaviours that support people's accountability. Examples include inviting trust, quality feedback and appropriate solutions.

Trust

Trust is the bedrock of positive relationships within the organisation. When we feel psychologically safe, we're more likely to trust those around us. Such trust not only encourages open communication and the sharing of insights but also fosters a culture of innovation and growth. When they're trusted, employees and colleagues show up as their best selves, leading to increased productivity and a more harmonious workplace.

Quality feedback

Quality and regular feedback nurtures personal and professional growth. It's vital for everyone to understand what they're doing well and how to improve through regular and open communication based on a culture of trust and respect. A positive, respectful workplace culture is critical for performance appraisal and management conversations that discuss individual goals, review achievements and set goals for the next feedback session or review. Equally, resources required to support individuals to do their work should be a focus, especially with access to mentors and coaches, and learning programs to build confidence and competence.

Solution-focused

Ron Carucci[45], who conducted a 15-year longitudinal study of more than 3200 leaders, has strongly argued that a solution-focused approach is key to fostering a collaborative and consultative process. A solution-focused conversation involving all stakeholders generates possible solutions to support the organisation's growth and development.

As the scenario below illustrates, those best involved in effective solution-focused activities will have healthy personal and professional efficacy, as well as a growth mindset.

Manager: 'Hi, team. I wanted to discuss our upcoming project. It's crucial that we all feel comfortable sharing our ideas and concerns. Trust is key to our success.'

Employee 1: 'Absolutely. When I know my input is valued and I'm not judged for mistakes, I feel more confident, which allows me to innovate.'

Employee 2: 'I agree. Last time, when we openly discussed our challenges, we found better solutions together. It really boosted our productivity.'

Manager: 'Exactly. Psychological safety allows us to take risks and learn from them. Let's ensure we maintain this environment by supporting each other and communicating openly.'

Employee 1: Thanks for emphasising this. It makes a huge difference in how we work and collaborate.'

Employee 2: 'Yes, knowing we have each other's backs helps us focus on delivering our best work.'

As we can see, accountability in the workplace is a cornerstone of productivity and success. However, each team member is responsible for effective communication, collaboration, respectful feedback and task completion.

But there's a difference between accountability and responsibility.

What is the difference between accountability and responsibility?

The figure below explains how accountability and responsibility differ.[46] Typically, one person is held accountable for ensuring the success of a project's desired outcomes or results. Responsibility differs slightly in that a person is held responsible for a specific task that contributes to the achievement of the overall project. In a project, responsibility is assigned to one or more individuals for completing specific tasks that contribute to the overall goals or outcomes of a project.

Accountability vs Responsibility

Accountability
- ✓ Ownership of results/outcomes
- ✓ Answerable for results
- ✓ One person
- ✓ Outcome-focused
- ✓ Held to account at the completion of a task
- ✓ E.g. submission of a quality report based on each team member's contribution

Responsibility
- ✓ Completion of assigned task or duty to individuals
- ✓ Shared
- ✓ Task-focused
- ✓ Held responsible before or during a task
- ✓ E.g. production of a report

What happens when there's a lack of accountability?

Team morale can suffer when it's hard to know who does what and what's important because roles and responsibilities are ambiguous or misaligned, as well as a team and organisation trying to function with unclear or conflicting priorities. Employee engagement is lowered because both personal and team objectives must still be achieved despite such hindrances.

Further exacerbating the problem are low levels of trust that are frequently associated with poor communication, lack of transparency and insufficient feedback loops. The challenges are compounded by limited resources – whether physical, social or capital – and unskilled leaders. Skilled leaders will maintain team morale because they manage staff effectively and provide the necessary support to help employees succeed in their roles.

Workplace accountability tools

I think we can agree that – in broad terms – we demonstrate accountability in the workplace when we:

- Complete assigned tasks within the agreed timeline and take responsibility for our team's success by offering support when needed

- Respect everyone's time by showing up prepared and punctual for meetings
- Take ownership of the problems we identify by proposing solutions and flagging issues when they arise without assuming someone else is handling them.

Of the tools available to support people to be accountable, I commend the DRI, the RACI Matrix and the Personal Accountability Ladder.

Directly Responsible Individual

The DRI, first used by Apple, refers to the person solely responsible for the success or failure of initiatives, activities and specific projects. Although they may not be working on projects alone, the DRI title means that the buck stops with them. They are responsible for task distribution, data collation, providing feedback and even sorting resources. They have a responsibility to collaborate and communicate with relevant stakeholders.

These individuals aren't just responsible for completing tasks but they are also empowered to get the job done. Their role is crucial in achieving critical outcomes. This approach focuses on the efficient achievement of the outcomes for which they're directly responsible.

The GitLab employee handbook explains how the DRI works in that organisation. Use the QR code to open the DRI section of GitLab's open-source handbook.

RACI matrix

The RACI matrix is a project management acronym for the different responsibility types within a project: Responsible, Accountable, Consulted and Informed. The tool clarifies roles for individuals in the delivery of the project by establishing assigned tasks within the agreed timeline.

The RACI example below illustrates how roles, responsibilities and expectations are distributed between team members. The RACI matrix establishes where team members must take ownership of problems and propose solutions. It's a proactive approach that ensures issues are addressed promptly by fostering an accountable and collaborative approach to problem-solving rather than simply flagging issues as they arise.

The RACI matrix is a road map that sets out a project's stages from start to finish, promoting accountability for those involved, whose roles and expectations are clearly identified. Such clarity is an enabling factor because people who have clarity about what is expected of them are more likely to take ownership of their tasks and contribute to the team's success.

RACI Matrix

	Dave	Bill	Anna	Kate	Cindy	Tanya	Susan	Peter	Tim
Planning / Schedule	R	A	I	C			Q		
Risk Management		I	I	Q	R			I	C
Quality Management			R	C			A		Q
Procurement	A			R			C		Q
1 Specifications Listing		R			A	Q	I		
2 Site Requirements		C	A	R		I	Q		
3 Call for Tenders		R		Q	I		C		I
4 Budget Approval	R				A	Q	C		
5 Contract Negotiations	I		A		C			R	

R: Resonsible (works on), A: Accountable, C: Consulted,
I: Informed, Q: Quality Reviewer

Personal accountability ladder

The personal accountability ladder helps us to examine our thinking and resulting behaviours. Bruce Gordon, a civil rights activist in the USA, developed it to shift people from a place in which they typically believe things happen *to* them and behave as the victim to a place where they believe things happen *because* of them, and they adopt proactive and accountable practices.

The ladder has eight rungs. The first four rungs highlight the path of the *powerless mindset* (Gordon's term) marked by a lack of awareness. Those with the powerless mindset blame, make excuses, and wait and hope. The next four rungs are the path of the *powerful mindset*, characterised by acknowledging reality, taking ownership, creating solutions and making things happen.

The ladder itself is powerful, offering us a step-by-step process to challenge our thinking and approaches to situations.

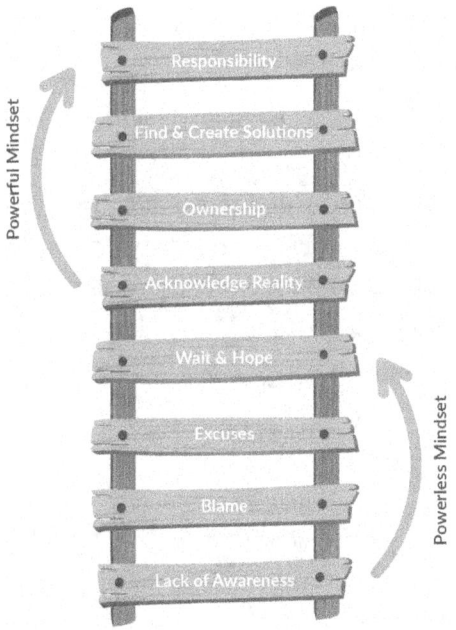

The DRI, RACI matrices and the personal accountability ladder are examples of tools that can be used as guides to reflect upon and reframe our thinking to be more accountable.

• • •

Chapter Six: Takeaways

This chapter began with the story of Everybody, Somebody, Anybody and Nobody to highlight that accountability belongs to all of us.

There are five key takeaways from this chapter.

1. **Everyone** is accountable.
2. The **two frames of accountability** are the conditions that foster accountability and the ownership of accountability.
3. Accountability and responsibility **aren't the same concept**.
4. Many **accountability tools** can be applied in the workplace. The DRI, RACI matrix and the personal accountability ladder are universally regarded as simple but powerful.
5. To be accountable and responsible in your place of work or personal life is to ...
    - Be you with *integrity*
    - Be you with *skill*
    - Be you with *courage*

Chapter Seven

Quality Decision-Making

• • •

Two Boats and a Helicopter [47]

A man sat on the roof of his house because there was a flood. The flood waters had risen to the level of the roof. There was grave concern that the floods would continue to rise. The man cried out to be saved. He waited a while, and a lifeguard swam over to the man's roof with a life jacket. The lifeguard said, 'Put this life jacket on and swim with me to safety.' The man replied, 'Thank you, but I am

waiting for God to save me.' The lifeguard swam away. A while later a rescue boat came and after that, a helicopter. The man gave the same reply each time. He stayed on the roof, and he drowned. He went to heaven and asked God, 'I prayed to you to save me, why didn't you save me?' God replied, 'What do you mean? I sent a lifeguard, a rescue boat, and a helicopter, and you refused them.'

• • •

The man sitting on the roof of his house, surrounded by flood waters, is a metaphor for someone who has a number of choices but doesn't act on any of them. An inability to make a decision could be attributed to a number of factors such as not seeing opportunities that come our way, relying on one way of thinking to the detriment of others, a failure to reflect or simply not taking action.

Decisions, decisions, decisions! We wake in the morning and make decisions throughout the day until we go to sleep. Decisions can be as easy as deciding whether it will be cereal or toast – or both – for breakfast, to decisions with more significant implications, such as ending a relationship, leaving a workplace or moving house. Our values and preferences influence the cognitive processes that lead to a decision. Decision-making is a skill that can be nurtured and learned.

What decisions need to be made to navigate the maze illustrated below? How many decisions, and what type of decisions, would you make?

Quality Decision-making

Amanda Reille[48] says that adults make between 33,000 and 35,000 decisions each day. Let's do some maths here. Assuming that the average person sleeps seven hours, we can calculate that 2000 decisions are made every hour while awake. That's approximately one decision every two seconds.

Decision-making tools

Have you ever made a decision with a coin toss or with the Stop Rule?

Coin toss

The humble coin toss for decision-making is a strategy when all options are equal. The outcome is usually acceptable to both parties. In fact, a random field experiment of participants who tossed a coin to decide something found they felt happy with their decision, even six months after the event.[49] There's a place for coin tossing as a strategy to make a decision, but there are people who prefer rationality and logical reasoning over randomness.

The Stop Rule

The Stop Rule relies on logical reasoning for decision-making.

The Stop Rule

Two variables of the stop rule:
non-negotiable limit (if we don't reach the summit by 2PM, we turn around)
and flexible limit (if my heart rate is below 150 by 2PM, I will keep climbing until 3PM)

The Stop Rule decision-making sets boundaries and establishes priorities that will inform a decision to stop pursuing an action. The framework simplifies decision-making, allowing individuals to align with personal and professional goals, consider multiple ideas and options, and reduce the stress associated with making a decision.

Three scenarios demonstrate the Stop Rule in action

1. An investor uses the Stop Rule to manage their stock portfolio. They set a rule to sell any stock that drops 15 percent below its purchase price. One of their stocks, initially performing well, starts to decline due to market volatility. When the stock hits the 15 percent loss threshold, the investor sells it, avoiding further potential losses. The Stop Rule, a disciplined approach, has helped the investor protect their overall portfolio and maintain financial stability.

2. A couple searching for their first home set a Stop Rule to avoid overextending their budget – if a house requires more than $50,000 in renovations, they won't proceed with the purchase. During their search, they find a charming house that seems perfect. However, after a thorough inspection, they discover that the necessary repairs and updates would cost around $60,000. Despite their emotional attachment to the house, they invoke their Stop Rule and decide not to buy it, ensuring they stay within their financial limits and avoid potential debt.

3. A single buyer sets a Stop Rule to prevent decision fatigue – if they haven't found a suitable home within six months, they'll pause their search and

reassess their criteria. After five months of looking at numerous properties, they still haven't found the right fit. As the six-month mark approaches, they decide to take a break, giving themselves time to reflect on their priorities and the market conditions. This Stop Rule helps them avoid burnout and make a more informed decision when they resume their search.

The 7-step decision-making process

In her YouTube video, Lauren Kress discusses seven steps to decision-making.[50]

1. Clarify and define the problem: what is it that needs to be addressed?

2. Determine the relevant goals: what goals need to be established and why?

3. Consider multiple solutions: what options are available to you?

4. Evaluate and compare each of the solutions: what is the value of each of the solutions brainstormed?

5. Based on the previous four steps, is the decision appropriate? Ensure that the criteria you have established to make the decision are met.

6. Implement the decision: once you've made the decision, what processes are required for its implementation?

7. Review the decision: how did the decision go? Did it address the issue or situation?

For people who like a scaffolded process, the seven steps guide sequences gathering and evaluating information for decision-making.

Consequences model[51]

The consequences model highlights what can happen when decisions aren't made in a timely manner. The model invites decision-makers to consider short-term and long-term consequences of their actions. By mapping out these consequences, individuals, teams and organisations can better understand the impact of their decisions and more more informed choices.

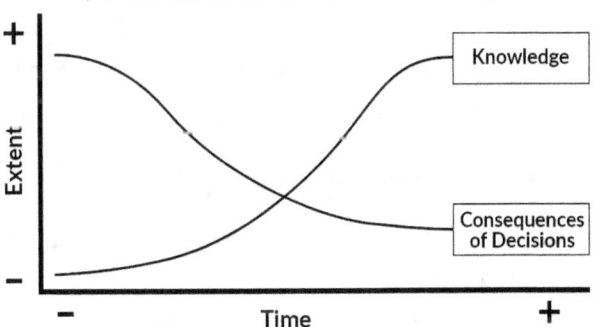

While the Consequences model offers a decision making process using tools and strategies, we cannot forget that making decisions also requires the acknowledgement of values and attitudes that influence decisions.

How do you prevent bias in decision-making?

In my first book, *It's All About IT! A guide to better communication and mastering conversation skills in the workplace*, I wrote about bias and its role in how we turn up for ourselves and others personally and professionally.

Cognitive bias is a real phenomenon. It is the amygdala's way of mitigating the large volume of information entering the brain. The amygdala compartmentalises content into categories, which simplifies the processing of information for the brain to make sense of. The problem, though, is that cognitive biases lead to errors in judgement that influence the way individuals understand events and make decisions.

Some indicators of cognitive bias in play are:

- Blaming others when things don't go the way you want
- Assuming that you know more than others
- Only noticing facts that confirm your way of thinking

- Assuming that everyone sees the world the same way you do.

Depending on your source of information, between 175 and 188 types of cognitive biases[52] can be identified. Let's acquaint ourselves with the three most commonly known: confirmation bias, attribution error and the halo effect.

Confirmation bias

This bias focuses only on facts and beliefs that support your own, as in the following situation.

Situation: Alex is considering investing in a new tech company, TechNova. He already believes that TechNova is a promising investment.

Confirmation bias in action
1. **Searching for positive information:** Alex primarily looks for articles and analysts' reports that highlight TechNova's potential for growth and innovation.

2. **Interpreting neutral information positively:** when Alex comes across a report that mentions both the strengths and weaknesses of TechNova, he focuses on the strengths and downplays the weaknesses.

3. **Ignoring negative information:** Alex dismisses or avoids reading reports that are critical of TechNova, such as those highlighting financial instability or market competition.

Outcome: *Alex ends up investing heavily in TechNova based on a skewed perception of its potential, influenced by his initial belief and the selective information he gathered.*

Attribution error

People make judgements or assumptions about other people's actions and link them to personal characteristics. A quality decision is at risk because that mindset and perspective influences how we see the other person.

Situation: Sarah is a manager at a marketing firm. One of her team members, John, misses a critical project deadline.

Attribution error in action

1. **Sarah's immediate reaction:** Sarah immediately thinks, 'John is lazy and irresponsible', attributing his missed deadline to his character.

2. **Ignoring situational factors:** Sarah doesn't consider that John might have faced unexpected challenges that prevented him from meeting the deadline, such as a family emergency or technical issues.

3. **Impact on decision-making:** based on her attribution, Sarah decides to give John a poor performance review, overlooking his previous track record of meeting deadlines and delivering quality work.

Outcome: *Sarah's judgement is clouded by the fundamental attribution error and delivers a potentially unfair assessment of John's performance. If she'd considered situational factors, she might have realised the missed deadline was an exception rather than a reflection of John's overall work ethic.*

The halo effect

The halo effect describes a decision made on the basis of a general judgement of a specific trait.

Situation: *Marie is exceptional at public speaking. Because of her impressive presentation skills, her manager assumes she's highly competent in other areas, such as project management or technical skills, despite no direct evidence of her proficiency in those areas.*

1. **Impact on decision-making:** the positive perception based on one outstanding trait can lead to Marie receiving more opportunities regardless of her actual performance in other aspects of her job.

2. **Increased opportunities:** Marie may receive more opportunities, such as leading projects or being assigned to high-visibility tasks, based on her perceived competence.

3. **Potential for misalignment:** if Marie lacks the necessary skills in project management or technical areas, these opportunities might not align with her

actual strengths, potentially leading to suboptimal performance.

4. **Resource allocation:** the manager might allocate resources and support to Marie, believing she can handle complex tasks, which could impact team dynamics and resource distribution.

5. **Employee development:** Marie might feel pressured to meet these expectations, which could either motivate her to develop new skills or lead to stress and job dissatisfaction if she struggles to perform.

6. **Team perception:** other team members might notice the bias and feel overlooked or undervalued, potentially affecting team morale and cohesion.

• • •

Chapter 7: Takeaways

Beliefs, values and mindsets influence decision-making and might impact others with short- and long-term consequences.

There are six key takeaways from this chapter.

1. Decision-making is a **cognitive process**.
2. Coin toss, the Stop Rule, the 7-step decision-making process and the consequences model are examples of **tools that aid decision-making**.
3. **Cognitive biases** can impact the decision-making process.
4. Confirmation bias, attribution error and the halo effect are **examples of cognitive biases**.
5. **Objective decision-making** includes evaluating our own beliefs, values and mindsets.
6. More than simply arriving at a decision, objective decision-making demands that you ...
   - Be you with *integrity*
   - Be you with *skill*
   - Be you with *courage*

Chapter Eight

Leadership with Integrity, Skill and Courage

• • •

Inspirational Leadership [53]

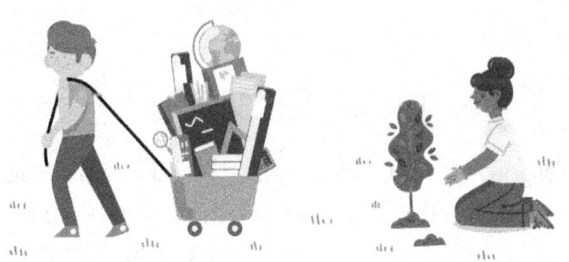

Zane Powles is a primary school teacher in Grimsby, a fishing port in Lincolnshire, on the east coast of England. During the global pandemic when schools were closed,

he noted that many of his students struggled to learn at home. With little access to technology and a focus on not wanting his students to miss out on learning, Zane walked eight kilometres every day to deliver homework tasks and provide them with packed lunches. He aimed to ensure that students felt safe when receiving the best education they could get under challenging circumstances.

Wangari Maathai was a Kenyan environmentalist who dedicated her life to caring for the environment and was well known for her advocacy of women's rights. As the founder of the Green Belt Movement in the 1970s, she worked to develop programs that focused on tree planting and environmental conservation, and educated world leaders on the importance of looking after flora and fauna. In 2004, Wangari became the first African woman to receive the Nobel Peace Prize for her work in sustainable development practices and women's rights.

• • •

Leadership as behaviour

Professor Amy Edmondson from the Harvard Business School points out that anyone can exercise leadership at any point in time by positively influencing others with leadership as a behaviour. Leadership is more than a position of authority. Zane Powles and Wangari Maathai demonstrated how leadership is about one's capacity to inspire and motivate others to engage with a purpose. Zane highlights the compassionate drive of one teacher who showed care for his students during a challenging global crisis. Wangari's passion and determination for the environment and women's rights overcame opposition, humiliation and verbal attacks.

Their leadership behaviour characterises the three-fold mantra repeated throughout this book: Be you with integrity, be you with skill and be you with courage.

Be you with integrity

Self-awareness empowers us to lead with integrity. Matt Mayberry, in an article with the intriguing title, 'You don't have to be the boss to be leader', emphasises self-awareness as an effective leadership behaviour.[54] Remember the flight attendants' instructions on an aircraft to fit your mask before you assist others? That's an analogy of what's being said here: develop yourself with a commitment to personal growth before attempting to assist others.

When self-aware, we lead with integrity because we're transparent about our values (Chapter 2), have increased capacity for emotional intelligence (Chapter 3), and have greater authenticity and resilience (Chapter 4).

Be you with skill

Skills required for effective leadership relate to the ability to engage and motivate (Chapter 5), be accountable (Chapter 6) and make quality decisions that are tested in reality (Chapter 7).

Underpinning these skills is the ability to connect with others through quality communication. Professor Edmondson has three criteria for communicational behaviour that exercises leadership at work.

The first is to frame the work by explaining in clear terms what's needed for a team to achieve a task. The second criterion for communication in leadership is to ask good questions. Asking thoughtful questions shows respect for others and invites their engagement and collaboration. The art of questioning and listening is an essential workplace skill to connect with people and accompany them on a journey of empowerment with an understanding of what they are thinking and feeling. The third criterion is to respond productively to the insights or contributions of others to learn and develop.

Peter Northouse[55] highlights communication as a leadership skill that fosters trust, accountability and psychological safety. Trust-filled relationships invite continuous development, foster curiosity, and take reasonable risks for long-term growth and development.

Be you with courage

It takes courage for self-aware individuals to acknowledge how their behaviours can impact others. It takes courage to acknowledge cognitive biases and commit to addressing and improving any areas of weakness.

The practice of leadership as behaviour takes courage because it demands we be vulnerable, authentic and empathic. [56]

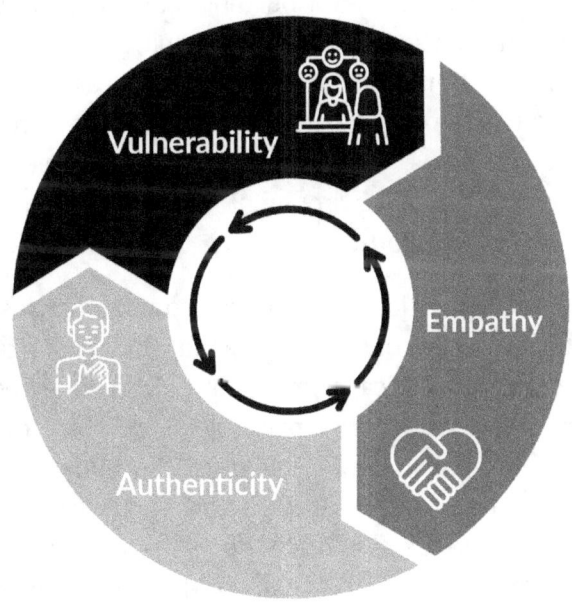

Circular Vulnerability

When vulnerable, we allow ourselves to acknowledge our thoughts and feelings even if they feel uncomfortable. Actionable vulnerability is when we recognise and own our mistakes and seek support to grow and develop.

Being authentic is about being genuine, being self-aware, and being willing to work with and accept others. Authenticity fosters trust and human connection.

Leadership without empathy is ineffective leadership. Empathy, understanding and appreciating the perspectives of others are not just soft skills – they're essential tools for building mutually reciprocal relationships. When we show genuine concern for others' emotions and experiences, we can connect with our team members, understand their needs and motivations, and generate a productive and harmonious work environment. Genuine concern is built through empathy.

Behavioural leadership takes courage because it forces us out of our comfort zone, our comfortable place of psychological safety. The comfort zone has its origins in the work of two psychologists, Robert Yerkes and John Dodson, who developed the eponymously titled law that is represented below. As psychologists, they were curious to explore the relationship between stress (or arousal, as they named it) and performance, highlighting the importance of balancing optimal stress with optimal performance. Performance increases with physiological or mental stress, but when stress levels become too high, performance decreases.

The Yerkes-Dodson Law of Arousal and Performance

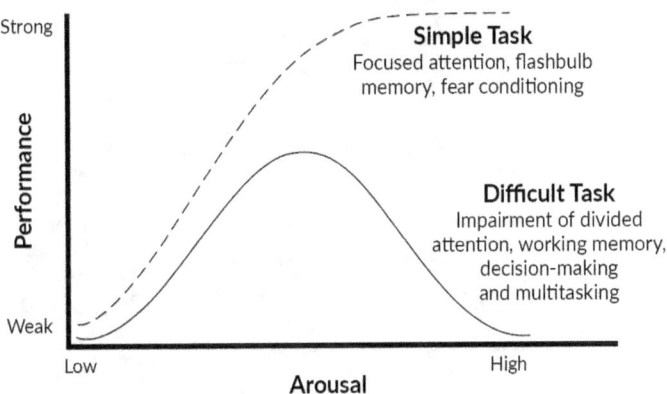

Our understanding of the comfort zone has developed since Yerkes and Dodson created it in 1908. The figure on page 112 shows us more clearly what happens in the comfort zone where we feel safe.[57] However, our capacity for personal or professional growth is reduced if we remain there. Moving outside the comfort zone into the fear zone is where we become vulnerable to anxiety and lack self-confidence. In the learning zone, we face our challenges and acquire new skills, which facilitates personal and professional growth in the growth zone. I like to call the growth zone the *eye* of growth because it's here that we set goals and work to achieve them. With newfound confidence and learning, we experience rewards.

Moving outside the Comfort Zone

Leadership as a way of being

Let me reiterate that leadership is a noun. Leadership involves behaviour. Leadership is a way of being, doing and relating as demonstrated by these individuals.

Greta Thunberg – as a 15-year-old climate activist, Greta contributed to the global movement for climate change, albeit creating worldwide headlines and commentary that wasn't always sympathetic to her actions. In 2018, Greta protested outside the Swedish parliament, seeking action on climate change. She inspired students to join Fridays for Future protests, skipping school to strike for climate change. Greta has addressed world leaders and international gatherings about the urgent attention required for climate change.

Malala Yousafzai survived an assassination attempt in Pakistan when Taliban fighters tried to kill her. Malala had protested the Taliban's policy prohibiting girls from going to school. Despite the assassination attempt, Malala refused to hide and continued to be the voice for the education of girls and women in Pakistan from the UK, where she underwent multiple surgeries to repair a bullet hole in her skull. Malala was awarded a Nobel Peace Prize in 2014 aged 17 for her courage and determination, becoming the youngest person in history to be awarded a Nobel Prize.

Nelson Mandela spent 27 years in prison for attempting to remove social segregation and discrimination in South Africa. After his release from prison in 1990, he continued to work with politicians and communities to dismantle apartheid. His influence and leadership led to his election in 1994 as the first black president of South Africa. Mandela's work transformed South Africa and inspired hope for global human rights and equality.

Dame Phyllis Frost and Colin Hill were disgusted by the litter in their local areas. They banded together in 1966 and created Australia's first national anti-litter and sustainability advocacy program, Keep Australia Beautiful. The program operates through all Australian territories and states with local initiatives, including school programs, to keep communities clean.

• • •

Chapter 8: Takeaways

Zane Powles, Wangari Maathai, Greta Thunberg, Malala Yousafzai, Nelson Mandela, and Dame Phyllis Frost and Colin Hill characterise leadership as behaviour. Their leadership demonstrated a capacity to inspire and motivate others to engage with a purpose.

There are seven key takeaways from this chapter.

1. Leadership is **more than** a position of authority.

2. **Anyone** can exercise leadership with leadership as behaviour.

3. **Leadership as behaviour** characterises the three-fold mantra repeated throughout this book: be you with integrity, be you with skill and be you with courage.

4. Self-awareness **empowers** us to lead with integrity.

5. An underpinning **skill for leadership** as behaviour is quality communication that fosters trust, accountability and psychological safety.

6. The practice of **leadership as behaviour** takes courage because it calls us to be vulnerable, authentic and empathic; we're forced out of our comfort zone.

7. Behavioural leadership is when you ...
    - Be you with *integrity*
    - Be you with *skill*
    - Be you with *courage*

PART 3

Call to Action

This final section is a call to action. What will you do to turn up for yourself, and what will you do to turn up for others effectively? What will you do to ...

- Be you with *integrity*
- Be you with *skill*
- Be you with *courage*

Chapter Nine

Tools and Techniques

• • •

Here you will find strategies for taking action to apply learning from this book. These strategies are not only easy to learn, but also easy to apply and adapt to your context.

Self-awareness

To explore self-awareness, consider the following:

- What motivates you?
- What drives you?

Journal

Commit to writing in a journal for 15 minutes every day. Reflect on your daily experiences with three questions:

- What did I do well today?
- What could I have improved today?
- What should I not do?

Consider the internal and external factors discussed in Chapter 1.

Meditation

Mindful meditation is another strategy you can use to learn more about yourself. Explore the many meditational tools and techniques to find a style of meditation that works for you.

Feedback from others

It's not always easy to hear feedback from others. However, you can set some boundaries and use the three wishes and a star framework.

Boundaries

Use boundaries to circle around your readiness to hear feedback. For example, at work, you might set boundaries with your line manager by explaining how you like to receive feedback. Feedback usually needs to be specific and timely, a balance of positives and negatives, and suggestions on how to improve performance.

Work example

Specific: During our last meeting, I noticed that you offered great suggestions to address the system blockage situation. However, there were a few instances when you stopped James from sharing his insights.

Timely: *I wanted to give this feedback now, while it's still fresh in our minds, so we can talk about what occurred.*

Balanced: *I respect your passion for all the projects we take on. It really keeps us afloat when the stakes are high. At the same time, it would be beneficial if you could work on allowing James to finish his points before you share your insights. This will ensure that James feels heard and respected.*

Supportive: *I appreciate your insights. Perhaps we can work on a system where you can refrain from jumping in and allowing James to share his thoughts. I'm more than happy to work with you on doing this so that team meetings are a positive experience for everyone.*

Three wishes and a star

The three wishes and a star framework for feedback is more personal. The three wishes highlight specific areas for improvement or change, and the star is the celebration of something being done well.

Work example

Your contributions to the volunteer group are valued and appreciated. Here are a few areas where I think you could improve.

(One wish) I wish you would be on time for our meetings so that you do not miss out on important information.

(Second wish) I wish you could follow through on the tasks given to you so that we can all fulfil the volunteer project requirements.

(Third wish) I also wish you could work on improving your attention to detail so that the reports are clear.

(The star) On a positive note, you have an uncanny ability to bring joy to the meetings and your positive attitude exemplifies a can-do attitude, which often reminds us about staying above the line and delving into negative thinking.

Values

What are your values? The values map and the values tree are two practical tools for exploring values.

Values map

A values map is a visual representation tool to identify core values. Depending on the design or format of the values map you choose, list the core values into categories and then order them by priority. When done well, the map will establish gaps or clashes in values and can be used to acknowledge any existing tension between innovation and security.

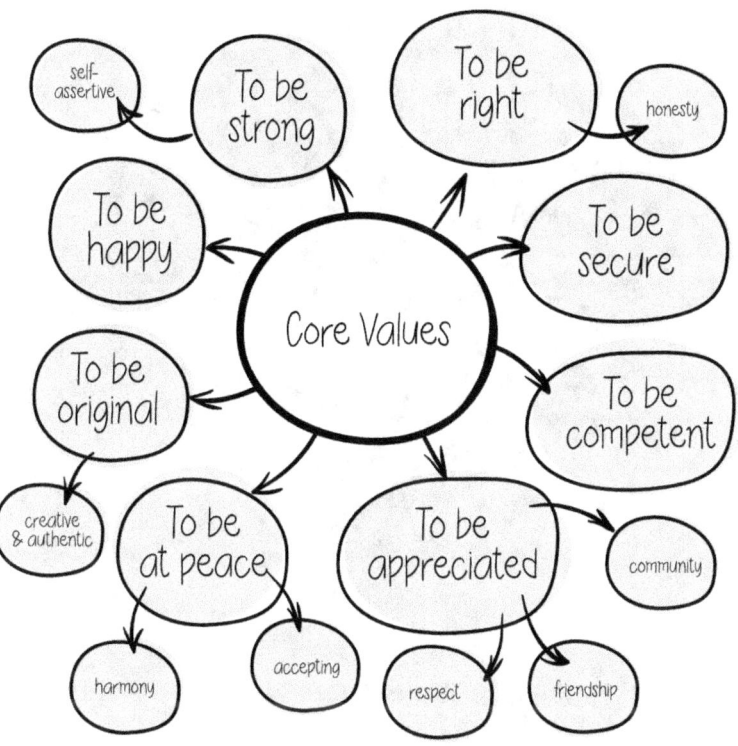

A values tree differs from a values map by refining the understanding of values. For example, the root system of the tree represents the core values. They are often non-negotiable and will guide decisions. The branches and leaves of a tree represent life and work categories. Values placed on the higher branches in each of these categories tend to be the most important. The overall structure of the tree links all the connections between the values.

Emotional intelligence

In Chapter 3, we learned that emotional intelligence is a multifaceted topic. We considered the importance of self-regulation and management, interpersonal skills, quality decision-making and a capacity to address stress. You might like to explore some of the following examples to help you develop emotional intelligence.

Self-reflection

Use some quiet time to address the following questions.

1. How often do I connect with people at home and work?

2. How do I develop strong relationships?

3. How do I react when faced with challenging situations?

4. What are my emotional triggers? How do they affect my behaviour?

5. What strategies do I use to regulate my behaviour?

6. How attuned am I to the needs and emotions of others?

7. How do I seek feedback from others about my responses to them?

8. What steps do I take to ensure effective communication with others?

Empathy building exercises

Role-playing scenarios explore the perspective of another person. Role-playing can be done with a trusted friend or colleague. Please make sure to set boundaries that respect the other person when doing this. It's always important that we honour the dignity of the human person, even if they're challenging us!

Empathy mapping[58] is used to understand the other person. There are four quadrants, each of which helps us to discern their thinking and general behaviour or their *why*. Draw a square with four quadrants and label them as shown in the example. Ask questions to explore what the person says, thinks, does and feels.

Says This quadrant provides insight into what the person needs, desires or is concerned about.	**Thinks** This quadrant seeks to understand the person's thoughts by linking to their motivations and internal conflicts.
Does This quadrant helps to consider the observed actions, behaviours and responses of the person.	**Feels** This quadrant seeks to understand the emotional state of the person.

Resilience

By understanding the individual and contextual risk and protective factors of any situation, we gain insights into how to strengthen resilience. Four strategies can help with this: a reflection quadrant, goal setting, learning new skills and reflection.

Reflection quadrant[59]

Reflect on your own individual risk and protective factors. For every individual risk factor, add a corresponding protective factor to mitigate the risk, as in this example.

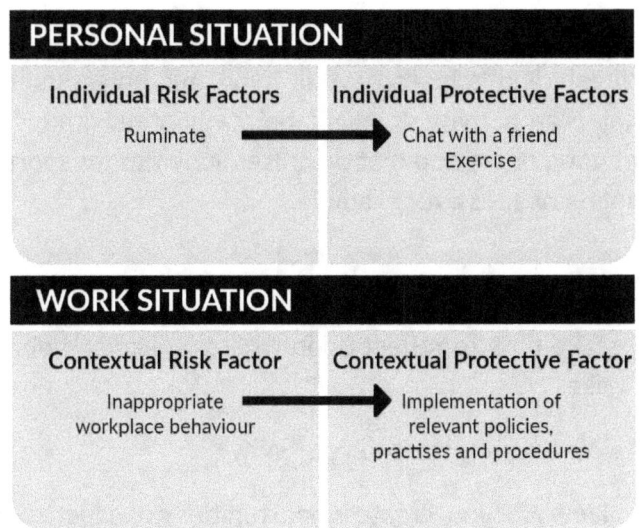

Goal setting

Respond in thoughtful ways to the following questions to begin setting goals.

1. What have you set out to achieve in the short-, mid- and long-term, both personally and professionally?
2. What do your goals look, feel and sound like?
3. What do you need to do more or less of?

SMART Goals

Specific   Measurable   Achievable   Realistic   Timely

Learn new things based on interest

Refresh and stimulate your mind and interests by joining an activity. It might be a volunteer group or network, or a group that organises activities for sports, gaming or chess, for example.

Reflection

1. Take time to reflect upon what you like and don't like.

2. What's important to you? Why?

3. How do you create opportunities to experience what's important to you?

Engagement and motivation

Team building exercises

Consistent workplace activities develop and strengthen employee relationships. These might include, for example, monthly sporting events, escape rooms, virtual scavenger hunts, lateral thinking puzzles and so on.

Wellness programs

Investigate your workplace. What's available to enhance employee satisfaction and productivity by promoting health and wellness? Consider these examples: flexible work arrangements, volunteer opportunities, mental health services, healthy eating initiatives, and on-site health programs such as flu shots and blood pressure assessments.

Accountability

Accountability in the workplace can be explored in creative but meaningful ways.

The hot seat

Team members of a task or project are invited to sit in the hot seat and answer questions about the project. It should be an activity that's fun yet with the serious intent of getting updated insights.

Five-minute stand-ups

At a meeting of all stakeholders in a project, each person has five minutes to share achievements or updates on the project component for which they are responsible.

Trust box

This is a space where staff can share challenges, concerns or feedback about a project anonymously. The information is written on a note and placed into the trust box for the entire team to resolve at a determined time.

Decision-making

As we learned in Chapter 7, despite making around 2000 decisions every hour, the quality of the decisions we make is important. Here are two ways to guide quality decisions.

Dot voting

Team members make decisions about various aspects of a project with, usually, differently coloured dot stickers. Participants vote on possible options for a decision by placing coloured stickers to indicate degrees of priority, which will determine priorities for action.

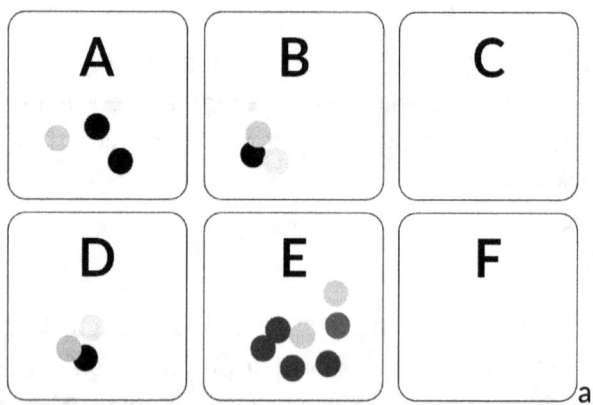
a

Effort/impact matrix[60]

Teams use this tool to prioritise tasks on the basis of the effort required to complete them and the impact that completion of the tasks might have. Decisions are based on low–high effort and low–high impact scales. Presumably, a team would make every effort to avoid thankless tasks (high effort but low impact)!

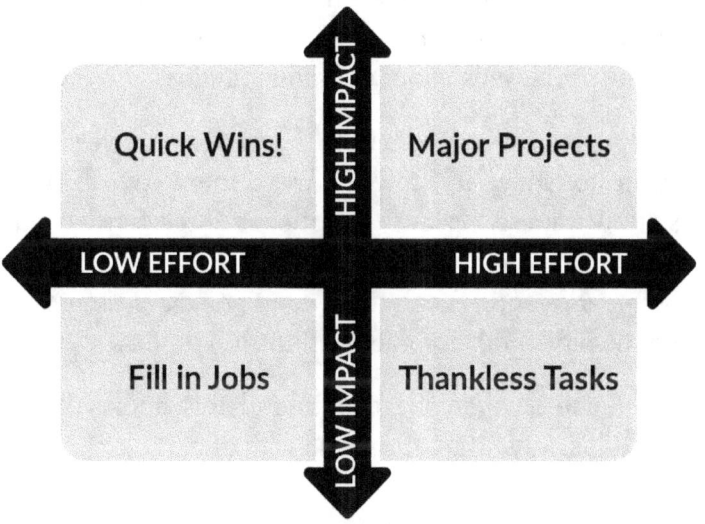

Bringing it all together

The tools and techniques offered here for formulating action plans are based on established learning principles that foster growth and development. They facilitate a proactive approach to being accountable and for nurturing a culture of continuous improvement through personal growth, engagement and commitment to others. They will not only develop your skills and abilities but also positively influence those around you.

Taking responsibility for being clear about our identity and personal conduct is important not just for ourselves, but also for those who spend time with us both at home and work. Taking responsibility is the foundation for identifying our objectives and our purpose, and directs us towards purposeful and respectful actions in our daily interactions.

As we show others how to treat us and welcome them to show us how to treat them, we exhibit self-awareness, values, emotional intelligence and resilience. Self-awareness, particularly in setting clear boundaries and expectations, can significantly improve the quality of our communication with others.

Since I began the chapters in this book with a story, it's only fitting that I end with one.

• • •

Tools and Techniques

The Frog in the Well

The Frog in the Well is a story with a philosophical lesson. It encourages us to consider what can happen when we go beyond what we know when we explore outside our comfort zone. The frog, confined to the limited perspective of the well, represents our self-imposed limitations. It's not until the frog meets a turtle from the sea, representing new experiences and perspectives, that the frog learns there's more to life. It's a tale about personal growth and self-awareness.

• • •

My wish is that you continue and engage in a journey of learning that's lifelong and rich with beautiful stories – stories of hope, stories that stretch, stories of perseverance, and above all, stories that encourage you to ...

- Be you with *integrity*
- Be you with *skill*
- Be you with *courage*

Endnotes

Introduction

1. I am using Goffee and Jones's ideas on how to be an effective leader with skill. Goffee, R., and Jones, G., (2019). *Why Should Anyone Be Led by You?*

Chapter One

2. Carden, J., Jones, R., & Passmore, J. (2022). *Defining self-awareness in the context of adult development: A systematic literature review.*

3. Australia Counselling. (n.d.) *What is Self-Awareness? How Does it Affect Me, and How Can I Improve?*

4. Rochat, P. (2015). *Layers of awareness in development.*

5. Taylor, C. (1989). *Sources of the self: The making of the modern identity.*

6. Eurich, T. (2018). *What self-awareness really is (and how to cultivate it?*

7. Waikar, S. 2019. *Microsoft CEO Satya Nadella: Be Bold and Be Right.*

8. See the video interview: Brown, B. & Ferris, T. (2020).

9. London, M., et al. Sessa, V. I., & Shelley, L. A. (2023). *Developing self-awareness: Learning processes for self-and interpersonal growth.*

10 Dweck, C. (2016) *What having a "growth mindset" actually means?*

Chapter 2

11 Monk, S. (2022). *Values, strengths and goals: How do they work together?*

12 Sagiv, L., & Schwartz, S. H. (2022). *Personal values across cultures.*

13 Guillemin, M & Nicholas, R. (2022). *Core values at work: Essential elements of a healthy workplace.*

14 Phillips, J.; Edwards, L. (2009) *Do you know what kind of commitment they have?*

15 Wrzesniewski, A.; et al. (2014) *Multiple types of motives don't multiply the motivations of West Point cadets.*

16 Clark, T. R. (2016). *Leading with character and competence: Moving beyond title, position, and authority.*

17 Lencioni, P. M. (2002). *Make your values mean something.*

18 Gleeson, B. (2021). *Why core values matter (and how to get your team excited about them?*

19 Waikar, S. (2019). *Microsoft CEO Satya Nadella; Be bold and be right.*

Chapter 3

20 Keltner, D., & Gross, J. (1999). *Functional accounts of emotions.*

21 Stein, S. J., & Book, H. E. (2011). *The EQ edge: Emotional intelligence and your success.*

22 Bughin, J. (2018). *Skill Shift: Automation and The Future of the Workforce.*

23 Bennett, M. (2023). *The Statistics on emotional intelligence in the workplace.*

24 Lee Hecht, Harrison & Penna. (2019). *EU: The great white whale of leadership development.*

25 Korn Ferry. (2021). *Emotional Intelligence: Why now?*

26 Lencioni, P. M. (2010). *The five dysfunctions of a team: A leadership fable.*

27 Royal Commission into Defence and Veteran Suicide (2024).

Chapter 4

28 Brown, B. (2013). *Daring greatly: How the courage to be vulnerable transforms the way we live, love, parent and lead.*

29 I've drawn on the following authors for the thoughts expressed here and elsewhere in this chapter: Beltman (2021). *Understanding and examining teacher resilience;* Bishop (2022), *Bouncing forward;* Goleman (2021), *Leadership: The power of emotional intelligence;* Hartmann et al. (2020), *Resilience in the workplace;* Lee & Duckworth (2018), *Organisational grit;* Luthans (2002), *The need for and meaning of positive*

organizational behaviour; Mansfield et al. (2012), *"Don't sweat the small stuff"*; McLarnon & Rothstein (2013), *Development and initial validation of the workplace resilience inventory.*

30 Hartmann, S., et al. (2020). *Resilience in the workplace.*

31 Beltman, S., et al., (2011). *Thriving not just surviving: A review of research on teacher resilience*

32 Ibid.

33 Citrin, R. S., & Weiss, A. (2016). *The resilience advantage: Stop managing stress and find your resiliencea*

Part 2

34 Mistry, P. 2017 *Richard Branson: 'Clients do not come first. Employees come first.'*

Chapter 5

35 Deci, E. L., & Ryan, R. M. (1985). *Intrinsic motivation and self-determination in human behavior.*

36 Bogyo, I. (2023). *Engagement and motivation: what is the difference?*

37 Kahn, W. A. (1990). *Psychological conditions of personal engagement and disengagement at work.*

38 Harter, J. K., et al., (2013). *The relationship between engagement at work and organizational outcomes.*

39 Ryan, R. M., & Deci, E. L. (2020). *Intrinsic and extrinsic motivation from a self-determination theory perspective.*

40 Berens, R. (2013). *The roots of employee engagement: A strategic approach.*

41 Cecchi-DiMeglio, P. (2024). *Six effective strategies to enhance employee engagement.*

42 Bolman, L. G., & Deal, T. E. (2014). *How great leaders think: The art of reframing.*

43 I've borrowed from the following authors for these ideas: Bolman & Deal, (2014). *How great leaders think*; Cecchi-Dimeglio, (2024). *Six effective strategies to enhance employee engagement.* Clark, (2020). *The 4 stages of psychological safety.*

44 Albercht, S. L., et al. (2015). *Employee engagement, human resource management practices and competitive advantage.*

Chapter 6

45 Carucci, R. (2022). It's time to overhaul our understanding of accountability. *https://handbook.gitlab.com/handbook/people-group/directly-responsible-individuals/*

46 I have adapted these ideas from *The Center for Leadership Studies.* (2024).

Chapter 7

47 Eternal Vigilance. (2012). *The parable of the flood.*

48 Reille, A. (2023). *A simple way to make better decisions.*

49 Levitt, S. D. (2016). *Heads or tails: The impact of a coin toss.*

50 Kress, L. *The 7 step decision making process.*

51 The decision Book by Mikael Krogerus and Roman Tschäppeler

52 Nortje, A. (2020). *What is cognitive bias?*

Chapter 8

53 Leadership stories *https://kapable.club/blog/leadership/leadership-stories/*

54 Mayberry, M. (2023). *You don't need to be 'the boss' to be a leader.*

55 Northouse, P. G. (2021). *Leadership: Theory and practice.*

56 Brown (2016). *Normalize the discomfort of learning and reframe failure as learning.*

57 Aikin-Smith, J. (2023). *Getting out of your comfort zone.*

58 Empathy Map modified from anadea.info (2025)

59 Adapted from https://www.lucidchart.com matrix/impact-effort (2025)

60 Adapted by Dr Nancy Bonfiglio-Pavisich (2025)

Bibliography

Aikin-Smith, J. (2023). *Getting Out of Your Comfort Zone: Challenging Yourself*. https://www.jamesakinsmith.co.uk/blog/comfort-zone/

Albercht, S. L., Bakker, A. B., Gruman, J. A., Macey, W. H., & Saks, A. M. (2015). Employee engagement, human resource management practices and competitive advantage: An integrated approach. *Journal of Organizational Effectiveness: People and Performance, 2,* 7– 35. doi:10.1108/joepp-08-2014-0042

Apple Newsroom Press Release (July 2020) – Apple commits to be 100 percent carbon neutral for its supply chain and products by 2030 - Apple

Arieli, S., Sagiv, L., & Roccas, S. (2020). Values at work: The impact of personal values in organisations. *Applied Psychology, 69(2), 230-275.*

Australia Counselling. (n.d.) *What is Self-Awareness? How Does it Affect Me, and How Can I Improve?*

Beltman, S. (2021). Understanding and examining teacher resilience from multiple perspectives. *Cultivating teacher resilience,* 11-26.

Beltman, S., Mansfield, C., & Price, A. (2011). Thriving not just surviving: A review of research on teacher resilience. *Educational research review,* 6(3), 185-207.

Bennett, M. : Apr 18, 2023 *The Statistics on Emotional Intelligence in the Workplace*, Niagara Institute https://www.niagarainstitute.com/blog/emotional-intelligence-statistics

Berens, R. (2013). The roots of employee engagement: A strategic approach. *Employment Relations Today*, 40, 43–49. doi:10.1002/ert.21420

Bishop, J. (2022). *Bouncing forward: Mental wealth for all. Medical Science Educator* 32(1), 59-514. https:??doi.org/10.1007/s40670-022-01692-w

Blog Post: *The Centre for Leadership Studies*, (2024). Building a culture of accountability.

Bogyo, I. (2023). *Engagement and motivation: what is the difference?* Effectory. What is the difference between employee engagement and motivation - Effectory

Bolman, L. G., & Deal, T. E. (2014). *How great leaders think: The art of reframing*. San Francisco, CA: Jossey-Bass.

Brown, B. (2013). *Daring greatly: How the courage to be vulnerable transforms the way we live, love, parent and lead.* London, England: Portfolio Penguin.

Brown, B. (2016). Brené Brown encourages educators to normalize the discomfort of learning and reframe failure as learning. *About Campus*, 20(6), 3-7.

Brown, B. and Ferris, T. (2020) Video Interview https://youtu.be/lRa_YuLu-9E?si=p4H6Sv-1INpulzJm

Bughin, J. (2018). *Skill Shift: Automation and The Future of the Workforce.* Mckinsey Global Institute.

Carden, J., Jones, R. J., & Passmore, J. (2022). Defining self-awareness in the context of adult development: A systematic literature review. *Journal of Management Education,* 46(1), 140-177, p. 143.

Carucci, R. (2022). *It's time to overhaul our understanding of accountability.* Forbes Newsletter

Cecchi-DiMeglio, P. (2024). *Six effective strategies to enhance employee engagement.* Forbes Publications.

Citrin, R. S., & Weiss, A. (2016). The resilience advantage: Stop managing stress and find your resilience. *Business Expert Press.*

Clark, T. R. (2016). L*eading with character and competence: Moving beyond title, position, and authority.* Berrett-Koehler Publishers.

Clark, T. R. (2020). *The 4 stages of psychological safety: Defining the path to inclusion and innovation.* Berrett-Koehler Publishers.

Collins, J. C., & Collins, J. (2006). *Good to great and the social sectors: A monograph to accompany good to great.* Random House.

Cruz, L. (2024) 100 team core values examples to help you build a strong company culture. *Clip Up,* March 29, 2024)

Dan Mall: *Choosing Between Two Good Options. How do you decide?* Published on 10 Feb 2023 at 10:04 AM https://danmall.com/posts/choosing-between-two-good-options/

Deci, E. L., & Ryan, R. M. (1985). *Intrinsic motivation and self-determination in human behavior.* New York, NY: Plenum.

doi/10.1073/pnas.1405298111 (accessed on 3 July 2022). [CrossRef] [PubMed

Dweck, C. (2016) What Having a "Growth Mindset" Actually Means. *Harvard Business Review* https://hbr.org/2016/01/what-having-a-growth-mindset-actually-means

Eds.; Pfeiffer: San Francisco, CA, USA, 2009. Available online: https://www.enterpriseengagement.org/Do-You-Know-What-Kind-of-Commitment-They-Have/Eurich, T. (2018). What Self-Awareness Really Is (and How to Cultivate It). *Harvard Business Review.* https://hbr.org/2018/01/what-self-awareness-really-is-and-how-to-cultivate-it

Eternal Vigilance. (2012). *The parable of the flood.* http://eternalvigilance.nz/2012/01/the-parable-of-the-flood/

Eurich, T. (2018). *What Self-Awareness Really Is (and How to Cultivate It).* https://hbr.org/2018/01/what-self-awareness-really-is-and-how-to-cultivate-it

Flaxington, B. (2019). Your values as a leader speak louder than you do. *Forbes Boston Business Council.*

Gleeson, B. (2021). Why Core Values Matter (And How To Get Your Team Excited About Them). *Forbes*. March, 30.

Goffee, R., and Jones, G., (2019). Why Should Anyone Be Led by You? https://hbr.org/2000/09/why-should-anyone-be-led-by-you

Golding, I (2017). Accountability: A story about four people named everybody, somebody, anybody, and nobody.

Goleman, D. (2021). *Leadership: The power of emotional intelligence*. More Than Sound LLC.

Guillemin, M & Nicholas, R. (2022). Elements of a healthy workplace. I*nternational Journal of Environmental Research and Public Health* 19, 1-17. https://doi.org/10.3390/ijerph191912505

Harter, J. K., Schmidt, F. L., Agrawal, S., Plowman, S. K., & Blue, A. (2013). *The relationship between engagement at work and organizational outcomes*. Gallup Poll Consulting University Press, Washington.

Hartmann, S., Weiss, M., Newman, A., & Hoegl, M. (2020). Resilience in the workplace: A multilevel review and synthesis. *Applied psychology*, 69(3), 913-959.

Harvard Business School GitLab Case Study Interview with GitLab CEO https://www.youtube.com/watch?v=jdN5mj5ieLk

https://www.forbes.com/sites/roncarucci/2022/06/04/its-time-to-overhaul-our-understanding-of-accountability/

Ingram, P., & Choi, Yoonjin, C. (2022). What does your company really stand for? Align what matters to you as an organisation with what matters to your employees. *Harvard Business Review*, November-December).

Kahn, W. A. (1990). Psychological conditions of personal engagement and disengagement at work. *Academy of Management Journal*, 33, 692–724.

Keep Australian Beautiful – Our Story Our Story - *Keep Australia Beautiful*

Keltner, D., & Gross, J. J. (1999). Functional accounts of emotions. *Cognition & Emotion*, 13(5), 467-480. (accessed on 3 July 2022).

Korn Ferry. (2021). *Emotional Intelligence: Why Now?* https://www.kornferry.com/institute/emotional-intelligence-why-now Accessed September 28, 2024.

Kouzes, J. M., & Posner, B. Z. (2023). *The leadership challenge: How to make extraordinary things happen in organizations.* John Wiley & Sons.

Kress, L. *The 7 step decision making process | Decision making model* | Lauren Kress https://www.youtube.com/watch?v=d53AFjxT5hQ

Lee Hecht Harrison and Penna (2019) *EQ: The Great White Whale of Leadership Development* https://

www.lhh.com/us/en/insights/eq-the-great-white-whale-of-leadership-development/ Accessed September 28, 2024.

Lee, T. H., & Duckworth, AL (2018). Organisational grit. Turning passion and perseverance into performance: the view from the health care industry. *Harvard Business Review* (September-October), 98-105.

Lencioni, P. M. (2002). Make your values mean something. *Harvard Business Review*, 80(7), 113-117.

Lencioni, P. M. (2010). *The five dysfunctions of a team: A leadership fable.* John Wiley & Sons.

Levitt, S. D. (2016). Heads or tails: The impact of a coin toss on major life decisions and subsequent happiness (No. w22487). *National Bureau of Economic Research.*

London, M., Sessa, V. I., & Shelley, L. A. (2023). Developing self-awareness: Learning processes for self-and interpersonal growth. *Annual Review of Organizational Psychology and Organizational Behavior*, 10(1), 261-288.

Luthans, F. (2002). The need for and meaning of positive organizational behaviour. *Journal of Organizational Behaviour*, 23(6), 695–706.

Mansfield, C. F., Beltman, S., Price, A., & McConney, A. (2012).'Don't sweat the small stuff:' Understanding teacher resilience at the chalkface. *Teaching and Teacher Education*, 28(3), 357-367.

Marfice, C. (2021). How teams can use the RACI matrix for collaborative success. https://www.spinach.ai/blog/communication/raci-matrix

Mayberry, M. (2023). You don't need to be "the boss" to be a leader. *Harvard Business Review Journal*. https://hbr.org/2023/02/you-dont-need-to-be-the-boss-to-be-a-leader

McKinsey & Co. (2023). *What is decision-making?* McKinsey Global Publishing

McLarnon, MJW, & Rothstein, M.G. (2013). Development and initial validation of the workplace resilience inventory. *Journal of Personnel Psychology*, 12(2), 63–73

Mead, G. H. (2023). *Self. In Social Theory Re-Wired* (pp. 425-437). Routledge.

Mistry, Priyansha, October 08, 2017 Richard Branson: 'Clients Do Not Come First. Employees Come First.' *The HR Digest* https://www.thehrdigest.com/richard-branson-clients-do-not-come-first-employees-come-first/

Monk, S. (2022). Values, strengths and goals: How do they work together? *Positive Psychology Blog* motivations of West Point cadets. Proc. Natl. Acad. Sci. USA 2014, 111, 10990–10995. Available online: https://www.pnas.org/

Nevin, S., Deacy, S., & Mackenzie, D. (2015). Alison Murray Hare and Tortoise. The Favourite Aesop's Fable.

Northouse, P. G. (2021). *Leadership: Theory and practice. Sage publications.*

Nortje, A. (2020). What is cognitive bias? 7 examples and resources. *Positive Psychology.com online*: https://positivepsychology.com/cognitive-biases/ (accessed on 23 January 2025). [CrossRef] [PubMed

Passarelli AM, Kolb DA. (2021). *The learning way: learning from experience as the path to lifelong learning.* See pp. 97–130 chrome-extension:// efaidnbmnnnibpcajpcglclefindmkaj/https:// learningfromexperience.com/downloads/ research-library/The-Learning%20Way-Learning-from-Experience-as-the-Path-to-Learning-and-Development.pdf

Phillips, J.; Edwards, L. Do you know what kind of commitment they have. In *Managing Talent Retention*; Phillips, J., Edwards, L.,

Rasheed, S. P., Younas, A., & Sundus, A. (2019). Self-awareness in nursing: A scoping review. *Journal of Clinical Nursing*, 28(5-6), 762-774. https://doi.org/10.1111/jocn.14708

Reille, A. (2023). A simple way to make better decisions. *Harvard Business Review.*

Richard Branson: 'Clients Do Not Come First. Employees Come First.' - *The HR Digest*

Ries, A. (2006). Understanding marketing psychology and the halo effect. *Advertising Age*, 17.

Rochat, P. (2015). Layers of awareness in development. *Developmental Review*, 38, 122-145.

Royal Commission into Defence and Veteran Suicide. (2024). *Final Report Volume 2: Serving the nation, and Defence culture and leadership.* https://defenceveteransuicide.royalcommission.gov.au/system/files/2024-09/final-report-volume-2.pdf

Ryan, R. M., & Deci, E. L. (2020). Intrinsic and extrinsic motivation from a self-determination theory perspective: Definitions, theory, practices, and future directions. *Contemporary educational psychology*, 61, 101860.

Sagiv, L., & Schwartz, S. H. (2022). Personal values across cultures. *Annual review of psychology*, 73(1), 517-546.

Schulte, P.; Vainio, H. Wellbeing at work: Overview and perspective. Scand. J. Work Environ. Health 2010, 6, 422–429. Available

Self Awareness: Key to Sustainable Leadership | *HuffPost Impact* (2017) https://youtu.be/Wh5SUF0gPWQ?si=SwKHGuHxSea3NB_o

Sidnell, J. (2021). Person and self. *The international encyclopedia of linguistic anthropology*, 1-13.

Stein, S. J., & Book, H. E. (2011). *The EQ edge: Emotional intelligence and your success.* John Wiley & Sons.

Stichter, M., & Saunders, L. (2019). Positive psychology and virtue: Values in action. *The Journal of Positive Psychology*, 14(1), 1-5.

Taylor, C. (1989). *Sources of the self: The making of the modern identity.* Harvard University Press.

Tennant, M. (2023). *The Power of Empathy: A Thirty-Day Path to Personal Growth and Social Change.* Chronicle Books.

The Center for Leadership Studies. (2024). Building a Culture of Accountability. https://situational.com/blog/building-a-culture-of-accountability/

Waikar, S. (2019). *Microsoft CEO Satya Nadella: Be Bold and Be Right.* November 26, 2019. https://www.gsb.stanford.edu/insights/microsoft-ceo-satya-nadella-be-bold-be-right Satya Nadella changed Microsoft's culture: how leaders can learn - Fast Company (06 03 2024)

What Is Cognitive Bias? 7 Examples & Resources (Incl. Codex)

White, E. (2022). Building a powerful mindset utilising the accountability ladder. Business Transformation Consulting Tips. https://www.cornerstoneagility.com/building-a-powerful-mindset-utilizing-the-accountability-ladder/

Wrzesniewski, A.; Schwartz, B.; Xiangyu, C.; Kane, M.; Omar, A.; Kolditz, T. Multiple types of motives don't multiply the motivation of West Point cadets. Proceedings of the National Academy of Sciences of the United States of America, 30 Jun 2014, 111(30):10990-10995 https://doi.org/10.1073/pnas.1405298111 https://europepmc.org/article/MED/24982165

For Further Reading

Advisorpedia https://www.advisorpedia.com/advisor-tools/accountability-a-story-about-four-people-named-everybody-somebody-anybody-and-nobody/

Amin, H. (2024). *How to make accountability a core part of your workplace culture.* Hypercontext. Accountability in the workplace means that all employees are responsible for their actions, behaviors, performance and decisions. It's also linked to an increase in commitment to work and employee morale, which leads to higher performance.

Barclay, K. (2021). *State of the field: The history of emotions.* History, 106(371), 456-466.

Brooks, C. (2024). *Emotional intelligence skills: How to spot them in hiring.* https://www.businessnewsdaily.com/15191-emotional-intelligence-hiring.html

Carucci, R. (2020). How to actually encourage employee accountability. *Harvard Business Review Magazine* https://hbr.org/2020/11/how-to-actually-encourage-employee-accountability

Caruso, K. (2024). *How does the brain make decisions? Mouse study provides insights into communication between neurons during decision-making.* Harvard Medical School

Cherry, K. (2024). Cognitive bias: common types and how to avoid them. *Explore Psychology, Cognitive Bias: Common Types and How to Avoid Them*

Cherry, K. (2024). *How to Boost Your Self-Awareness.* Verywell Mind1.

Cleveland Clinic https://my.clevelandclinic.org/health/body/24894-amygdala

Copenhagen, Denmark; 26–28 May 2014. Available online: http://www.robinnicholas.com/index.php/beyond-the-intellectcommunicating-core-values-to-support-worker-wellbeing/(accessed on 3 July 2022).

Côté, S. (2014). *Emotional intelligence in organizations.* Annu. Rev. Organ. Psychol. Organ. Behav., 1(1), 459-488.

Edmondson, A. C., & Bransby, D. P. (2023). Psychological safety comes of age: Observed themes in an established literature. *Annual Review of Organizational Psychology and Organizational Behavior*, 10(1), 55-78.

Haidt, J. (2006). *The Happiness Hypothesis: Finding Modern Truth in Ancient Wisdom*

Haines, V. Y., & St-Onge, S. (2012). Performance management effectiveness: Practices or context? *The International Journal of Human Resource Management*, 23, 1158–1175. doi:10.1080/09585192.2011.561230

Harter, J. K., Schmidt, F. L., Agrawal, S., Blue, A., Plowman, S. K., & Josh, P., & Asplund, J. (2020). *The relationship between engagement at work and organizational outcomes.* Gallup Poll Consulting University Press, Washington.

Harvard Business Review (2019). *The EI Advantage: Driving Innovation and Business Success through the power of emotional intelligence.*

Jacobson, A. (2021). *Emotional intelligence: A simple and actionable guide to increasing performance, engagement and ownership.* John Wiley & Sons.

Kegan R.1994. *In Over Our Heads.* Cambridge, MA: Harvard Univ. Press

King, D. D., Newman, A., & Luthans, F. (2016). Not if, but when we need resilience in the workplace. *Journal of organizational behaviour,* 37(5), 782-786.

Kolb DA, Fry R. 1975. *Toward an applied theory of experiential learning.* In Theories of Group Process, ed. C Cooper, pp. 33-57. London: John Wiley

Krogerus, M., Tschäppeler, R., & Earnhart, P. (2012). *The decision book: 50 models for strategic thinking.* WW Norton & Company.

Laske OE.1999. *An integrated model of developmental coaching.* Consult. Psychol. J. 51:139-59

Lowe, G. (2012). How employee engagement matters for hospital performance. *Healthcare Quarterly,* 15, 29-39. doi:10.12927/hcq.2012.22915

Markos, S., & Sridevi, M. S. (2010). Employee engagement: The key to improving performance. *International journal of business and management*, 5(12), 89.

May, E. (2023). The statistics on emotional intelligence in the workplace. https://www.niagarainstitute.com/blog/emotional-intelligence-statistics

Mayer, J. D., Salovey, P., & Caruso, D. (2002). Mayer-Salovey-Caruso-Emotional-Intelligence Tests (MSCEIT) User's Manual (Toronto: Multi-Health Systems Inc.,

McLeod, S. (2023). https://www.simplypsychology.org/schachter-singer-theory.html

Mind the Gap: *The essential guide to workplace accountability.* chrome-extension://efaidnbmnnnibpcajpcglclefindmkaj/https://saanys.org/wp-content/uploads/2020/10/Mind-The-Gap-The-Essential-Guide-to-Workplace-Accountability-Ebook.pdf

Mograbi, CD, Hall, C., Arantes. B., Huntley, J. (2023). *The cognitive neuroscience of self-awareness: Current framework, clinical implications, and future research directions.* Wiley, 1-15.doi/10.1002/wcs.1670

Morris, L. S., Grehl, M. M., Rutter, S. B., Mehta, M., & Westwater, M. L. (2022). On what motivates us: a detailed review of intrinsic v. extrinsic motivation. *Psychological medicine*, 52(10), 1801-1816.

Nicholas, R. *Beyond the intellect: Communicating Core Values to Support Worker Wellbeing*. Presented at Wellbeing at Work,

Nicholas, T. W., & Erakovic, R. (2013). Authentic leadership and implicit theory: A normative form of leadership. *Leadership & Organization Development Journal*, 34, 182–195. doi:10.1108/01437731311321931

Nienaber, H., & Martins, N. (2020). Exploratory study: Determine which dimensions enhance the levels of employee engagement to improve organisational effectiveness. *The TQM Journal*, 32(3), 475-495.

Osborne, S., & Hammoud, M. S. (2017). Effective employee engagement in the workplace. *International Journal of Applied Management and Technology*, 16(1), 4.

Penn State: *Psychology of human emotion: an open access textbook* https://psu.pb.unizin.org/psych425/chapter/is-it-an-emotion/

Rees, C. S., Breen, L. J., Cusack, L., & Hegney, D. (2015). Understanding individual resilience in the workplace: the international collaboration of workforce resilience model. *Frontiers in psychology*, 6, 73.

Rigoni, B, & Nelson, B. (2016). *Do employees really know what is expected of them*. Gallup Business Journal (September 27)

Rochat, Philippe (2003). Five levels of self-awareness as they unfold early in life. *Consciousness and Cognition 12* (4):717-731

Rock, D., Sarro, E., & Weller, C. (2024). 3 ways to compassionately hold your team accountable. *Harvard Business Review* Publishing

Salovey, P., & Pizarro, D. A. (2003). *The value of emotional intelligence* (pp. 263-278). n.a.

Schwartz, S. H. (2012). An overview of the Schwartz theory of basic values. *Online readings in Psychology and Culture*, 2(1), 11.

Shahid, A., & Azhar, S. M. (2013). Gaining employee commitment: Linking to organizational effectiveness. *Journal of Management Research*, 5, 250–268. doi:10.5296/jmr.v5i1.2319

Sharma, R. (2010). *The leader who had no title: a modern fable on real success in business and in life.* Simon and Schuster.

Stein, S. J., & Book, H. E. (2011). *The EQ edge: Emotional intelligence and your success.* John Wiley & Sons.

Sutton A., Williams H. M., Allinson C. W. (2015). A longitudinal mixed method of self-awareness training in the workplace. *European Journal of Training and Development*, 39(7), 610-627. https://doi.org/10.1108/EJTD-04-2015-0031

Teimouri, H., Chegini, M. G., Jenab, K., Khoury, S., & LaFevor, K. (2016). Study of the relationship between employee engagement and organisational effectiveness. *International Journal of Business Excellence*, 10(1), 37-54.

Vallerand, R. J. (2012). From motivation to passion: In search of the motivational processes involved in a meaningful life. *Canadian Psychology*, 53, 42–52. doi:10.1037/a0026377

Vandenabeele, W. (2014). Explaining public service motivation: The role of leadership and basic needs satisfaction. *Review of Public Personnel Administration*, 34, 153–173. doi:10.1177/0734371x14521458

Yarwood, M. G. (2022). *Psychology of Human Emotion: An Open Access Textbook*. Affordable Course Transformation, Pennsylvania

www.ingramcontent.com/pod-product-compliance
Lightning Source LLC
Chambersburg PA
CBHW071241070526
44583CB00017B/2286